What BOARD GAMES Mean to Me

Edited by
Donna Gregory

Featuring contributions from

Edoardo Albert
Jenn Bartlett
Alessio Cavatore
Matt Coward-Gibbs
Jack Doddy
Christopher John Eggett
Geoff Engelstein
Matt Forbeck
Donna Gregory
Steve Jackson
Jervis Johnson
Reiner Knizia
John Kovalic
Sen-Foong Lim

Ian Livingstone
Will McDermott
Susan McKinley Ross
Holly Nielsen
KC Ogbuagu
Lynn Potyen
Gabriela Santiago
Fertessa Allyse Scott
Leslie Scott
Allen Stroud
Gav Thorpe
James Wallis
Cathleen Williams
Calvin Wong Tze Loon

Also Available in the Play to Win Series

Everybody Wins: Four Decades of
the Greatest Board Games Ever Made

By James Wallis

HARDCOVER • EBOOK • AUDIOBOOK

What
BOARD
GAMES
Mean to Me

Edited by
DONNA GREGORY

First published by Aconyte Books in 2023
ISBN 978-1-83908-272-6
Ebook ISBN 978-1-83908-271-9

Part of the PLAY TO WIN series from ACONYTE BOOKS
Editor: Donna Gregory
Cover & Book Design: ABC Design

Distributed in North America by Simon & Schuster Inc, New York, USA
Printed in the United States
9 8 7 6 5 4 3 2 1

ACONYTE BOOKS
An imprint of Asmodee Entertainment Ltd
Mercury House, Shipstones Business Centre
North Gate, Nottingham NG7 7FN, UK
aconytebooks.com // twitter.com/aconytebooks

CONTENTS

Editor's Note

The authors of this book are from all over the world and in some cases refer to the same game by different names. For example, checkers is known as draughts in the UK, while *Clue* is known as *Cluedo* outside of North America. In each individual piece, we have preserved the author's preferred name for the games they talk about, and provided the alternative names for clarity where necessary. If you're curious about any of the games mentioned in this book, we recommend visiting BoardGameGeek.com – a vast, comprehensive and up-to-date online database of more than 100,000 board games.

INTRODUCTION

Donna Gregory

Everyone's played a game or two at some point, even if only a round of *Monopoly* at a relative's house during the holidays or a decades-old copy of *Trivial Pursuit* on a rainy afternoon. Board games have been around for a long time but over the last four decades there has been an explosion in the number and types of games available to play. There has also been a proliferation of board game cafés and friendly local games stores in cities and towns all over the world. Games night is as much a staple of many modern social lives as a dinner party or a trip to the cinema. Hollywood stars such as Dax Shephard and Kristen Bell skip the post-red carpet parties to go home and play *CATAN*. BoardGameGeek has more than 100,000 games listed, and crowdfunding platforms such as Kickstarter have made it easier than ever for new, and often independent, designers and publishers to publish their games. The board games industry is projected to grow from US$15 billion in 2021 to US$34 billion by 2030, and has spawned several thriving sub-industries, including podcasts, websites, accessories and more. What's behind all of this is a story for another book but it's clear that board games mean much more than mere child's play to a great number of people.

When approaching people to contribute to this book, it became apparent that almost everyone who loves games values them as a way to spend quality time with people they like. Games remind us of the good times with our friends and family – we tend to play when we're relaxed, happy and have time to spend with people we like. In today's busy world, free time is precious and the options for spending that time are infinite. TV, video games, fitness, sports, reading, DIY and social media are all huge draws for most people, and yet the number of board games people play and the amount of time they spend playing them is only increasing. Board games must be giving us something we're not getting elsewhere.

So, it's clear that board games mean something – but they don't mean exactly the same thing to any two people. This book contains a collection of stories from a wide range of people, each telling us what board games mean to them. There are some common themes, and the stories told in this book are grouped into five themed sections, Life, People, Places, Play and Winning and Losing – though neither the sections, nor the individual essays within them, need to be read in order. Some of the stories in this book are written by games designers, publishers and industry experts but others are by people from all walks of life. Of the industry professionals, some talk about their work in the games industry while many have chosen to discuss the more personal stories in which they are simply gamers. The other contributors to this book include writers, a stay-at-home parent, a librarian, parents of children with additional needs, academics, an actor and more – and all have stories to tell about how board games have affected their lives, work and relationships in sometimes surprising ways.

Nowadays, many thousands of people make their living from board games, something which would have been unthinkable just a few decades ago, and in this book you'll find contributions from some of the pioneers and big names in the industry, as well as many younger talents. Reiner Knizia talks about his design process, as well as some fascinating thoughts on the rise of solo gaming. Fertessa Allyse Scott recounts the story of how she designed her first ever game with crafting supplies bought in her lunch break. Jervis Johnson tells the tale of how he discovered that games could offer some reassuring structure to his younger, somewhat anxious self, while Alessio Cavatore talks frankly about how it feels to receive criticism through the development and release of a new game.

We are often introduced to games by our family members. The importance of games to Susan McKinley Ross's relationship with her mother led her to develop one of the world's most popular games, *Qwirkle*. Gabriela Santiago tells the story of how board games helped her to navigate a tricky stage in her relationship with her younger, far-away half-siblings. *Jenga* inventor Leslie Scott writes about how the fond memories made playing games with people she loved have stayed with her long after the people themselves are gone. Novelist Will McDermott writes about how important games nights are to him, both with friends and family. Geoff Engelstein tells the story of how, after moving to a new school, he managed to make a new friend by fixing a broken old board game. For my own part, board games have always been the most reliable way to make new friends after moving house, something I've done a lot throughout my life, as I talk about in the section on Places.

Games can be more than just a fun way to pass an evening with friends. Author and historian Edoardo Albert recounts how board games were a crucial part of learning to communicate with his autistic sons, and how one of them took his love of *Ticket to Ride* to surprising ends. Games store owner Lynn Potyen writes about how her experiences with a speech therapist who used board games to help her son with a speech delay led her to open a store and to use games to help people with all sorts of brain differences or illnesses, from Alzheimer's to autism. And librarian Jenn Bartlett talks about how an idle thought in the shower one day led her to start a board games project at her library.

The essays in this book tell the story of what board games mean to a whole host of individuals, but together they give a broad-ranging view of why board games have become such an important part of popular culture. We imagine that, as a reader, among the different experiences described by our contributors, you'll find many that you share and can relate to, but also some unfamiliar perspectives as well. We hope that all of these stories will set you thinking about what board games mean to you, too.

Donna Gregory
Scotland, August 2023

LIFE

THE VOICE OF THE MUMMY

Geoff Engelstein

Susan pulls the game out of her closet. "If you fix it, we can play it."

It is 1977, we're thirteen years old, and in her room.

The game in question is *Voice of the Mummy*. The hook of the game is that there is a small vinyl record inside the game board, and the Mummy tells you what to do, as you move around and collect gems.

I don't remember why I was at Susan's house. I do remember that I was freaking out inside. I had moved into town a few months prior, and it was the first time I had moved, so it was a new experience. I was not great at making friends.

Like most of you, probably, I was particularly shy and awkward at thirteen. I was not athletic, a little weird, and a lot nerdy. Not a great combination for social acceptance.

Fortunately, I quickly fell in with a nice group of friends, all of whom were a little bit more athletic than I was, a little bit less weird, and mostly not nerdy at all. The most popular of my new friends was Susan. She was funny and smart and beautiful. To me, Susan was the epitome of middle-school cool.

While we were in the same social circle, we weren't that close. But somehow I ended up at her house. Maybe we were working on a school project? Let's go with that.

I had never hung out one-on-one with Susan before. What would we talk about? How long could I keep up the conversation before I said something stupid? So I asked, "Do you want to play a game?"

She agreed, and opened the closet where her games were stored. Most were staples of the 70s, but I had never seen *Voice of the Mummy* before, so I suggested we try that.

Turns out the record player had been broken for years. But she took it out and said, "If you can fix it, we can play it."

Image: Luis Rosas

A smarter person probably would have just suggested we play something else. But I had messed around with electronics a little bit – a very little bit – and decided that this was my opportunity to impress her. Maybe I couldn't throw or catch, but this was at least something that might work out.

I've spent a lot of time thinking analytically about games and what makes them tick. While I love mechanics (heck, I even co-wrote a 600-page encyclopedia about them), the more I play, observe and analyze games, the more I realize that games are about creating a space for social interaction – for people.

If you're socially anxious (like I definitely was at thirteen, and am still now to a certain extent), being at a party or at Susan's house is a tough situation. How do you go up to people and start talking to them? How do you talk to complete strangers?

This type of unstructured interaction can be really anxiety-inducing for many people. But a game, by its very nature, defines how we can interact. There are steps and actions we take. There is a common topic of conversation we can always fall back on – what's going on in the game.

Some games, like the cooperative family game *Hanabi*, even regulate the words that you're allowed to say.

If you are running a party or event where people don't know each other, often you'll start with an icebreaker. These icebreakers are always games. They create a structure that makes it easier for people to interact with each other.

This is why I suggested to Susan that we play a game. When I'm anxious in a social situation, I instinctively reach out for a game, something that will define what we do while we're hanging out.

I disassembled *Voice of the Mummy* and got to the record player. With Susan peering over my shoulder, I traced through the wiring and saw that one of the connecting wires had frayed and broken. In short order I was able to splice it back together, and the Mummy had a voice once more.

My gamble paid off. She was duly impressed. We played the game and, while it wasn't particularly complex or absorbing, we had a good time and laughed throughout.

We were thirteen years old at the time. Thirteen years later we got married.

To me, games aren't about mechanics or art or theme. They're about the way they bring people together and give them experiences they remember for a lifetime.

GEOFF ENGELSTEIN *is an award-winning table-top game designer and educator, whose titles include* Space Cadets, The Expanse, *and* Super Skill Pinball. *He has written several books, and is also a noted podcaster. Geoff is an adjunct professor of game design at the NYU Game Center. He has degrees in Physics and Electrical Engineering from the Massachusetts Institute of Technology, and is the president of Mars International, a design engineering firm.*

PICTURE A SCENE

KC Ogbuagu

A Beginning

It's a beautiful evening in the village, a cool breeze evident in the movement of tree branches and palm fronds. There are the sounds of chickens in the background and the occasional bleat from the goat house. There are small groups of adults smiling and talking as they carry out routine tasks in various corners of the village and then there is a group of children playing outdoors: my cousins, siblings and me.

We only see each other during the Christmas holidays, when we all travel back from the city to the village, and we are consumed with joy. We love getting up to mischief or playing games together, and to the despair of every adult in our extended family who would like us to keep our "nice" clothes clean, we usually play on the floor outside. On this particular evening, our chosen activity is a game of *ncho*, known elsewhere as mancala.

You see, in the city, we had the wooden version of the game with pebbles, but it was more exciting to play with stones found on the floor on a board that we traced in the dirt. Looking back, I wonder if it was fun because of the Christmas season or whether it was because of the joy that came from playing with our much-missed cousins; well, we will never know.

Another of my early gaming memories begins in an elementary classroom filled by thirty-five children with an average of seven years old. Seated at the desk at the far end of the third row is an eight year-old me, neatly clothed in a red-and-yellow striped shirt tucked into dark red shorts. On the desk is a collection of rubber bands mischievously hidden with my notebook as I jot down what our class teacher writes on the blackboard – or so she, and everyone else, thinks.

But in truth, I am playing an interesting and very popular game among the kids in my country called "Rubber." Rubber is a simple game that basically involved taking turns to throw rubber bands on the floor, trying to get them to land on top of each other. If your rubber band landed atop another child's rubber band, you got to keep both rubber bands. The best players would end up wearing rubber bands all the way up their arms to their elbows. We played Rubber in the classroom even when there were dire consequences like being flogged. We played Rubber on the streets even when we were banned from playing on the dirt. We played Rubber in churches and anywhere else we could find a rival. We played constantly, and it was fun!

These two particular scenes from my life have played back over and over again in my mind. Now, as a games designer, I remember the feeling I had as a child every time I finish a new prototype. When I see a kid playing one of my games, I can't help but smile as I remember that feeling. When I support someone to release their own games, I remember that feeling.

Defining Moment

The first big step on my journey to the tabletop gaming world was in 2013, on the campus in the old city of Calabar in Cross River State, Nigeria. Due to a disagreement with the government, the academic staff union embarked on an indefinite strike which eventually lasted for six months. While we were on strike, I promised a friend I would design a game for them. Prior to making such a promise, I had never designed a game before. In fact, I knew so little about games that I didn't know there were other types of dice apart from D6 (six-sided dice). I knew very little about board games other than the old classics like chess, *Whot!*, Ludo, *Monopoly*, *Scrabble* and, of course, ncho. I still do not know why I made such a commitment.

Within a month, my prototype was ready – I call it a prototype now, but this was "the game." It was everything I thought it could be at the time. Stones for tokens, two dice from a Ludo set, a couple of pieces of poorly cut paper as cards, and a rolled-up cardboard sheet for the board. *Ukubuwa* was born. My first board game! But something happened to me, something that I had never experienced before, something I didn't expect: I was fulfilled.

I can't explain it – I was so satisfied to have made a real board game. I never, ever thought of mass production or selling the game rights. It didn't occur to me. I didn't even know it was possible! When I saw people playing it for the first time, my twenty-one year-old self had found what I wanted to do for the rest of my life. I couldn't explain it fully then and I still can't explain it fully now.

Another Moment

Fast-forward to 2015. A new scene. It's dusk in the city of Ikorodu, Lagos State. The streets and the houses are busy with activity. In the sitting room of one of the apartments of a newly built milk-colored one-story building is a group of twenty-one young people; a third of them are from the UK, another third from Kenya, and the rest from different parts of Nigeria. I am not among the twenty-one young people. I am one of the three team leaders, each representing one of the countries. We are there to provide supervision and support for this group of diverse young people who have volunteered to support learning for children in some schools and on the streets.

We have just finished a meeting (these almost always involve settling conflicts between individuals or working groups). At the end of this particular meeting, everyone is agreed that we should host a social hangout to calm nerves and foster unity. One of the planned activities for the hangout is playing games. I don't fully realize what kinds of "games" we will be playing until I see the card games some of the UK volunteers have brought with them. This is my second defining moment.

At first, I was shocked, then I was amazed, then amazement turned to excitement. "This is the best group so far to share my games with," I said to myself. Over the years, I had taken my game prototype from campus with me on trips and showed it to anyone who was interested. I guess it meant so much to me – so I brought out the worn-out prototype and explained the idea behind the design and also taught the game. The volunteers, including my counterpart team leaders, were surprised that I had designed a game. It was apparently a difficult task and usually takes a lot of processes to design, develop and publish a game. I was hugely inspired and now, a purpose I had found two years earlier had taken a huge push forward, even if that push was only psychological at the time. As you can imagine, they shared a lot of feedback, and some fun memories of playing other games.

After playing my game, a crazy thing happened. They requested that I design another game with more details, like playing time, number of players the game could accommodate, and a theme. For the second time, I made another commitment and three weeks later I had designed a new game based on a childhood Nollywood movie. By the end of the three-month volunteering time, I had designed two more games. That was the beginning of what became NIBCARD Games, a tabletop games company that has gone on to manufacture and published forty-five of my games, manufactured twenty-two more games for clients from two different continents, hosted a yearly tabletop games convention (arguably the first in Sub-Saharan Africa) since 2016, and opened the first tabletop games café in Nigeria.

Daring to Build

NIBCARD Games' journey has been one of highs and lows, but one thing about a journey is that you are never stagnant. I remember walking the streets of Ikorodu in 2015 dreaming of people playing my games all over the world. That was all I wanted, but I guess the saying, "if wishes were horses, beggars would ride," is true after all.

Gradually, it became clear that I had to build my own ride. First, I had to learn some graphic design skills, since I had no access to capital to pay professionals to work on my ideas. The reality was that board game design had never been done locally before, which made it difficult to explain to people what I wanted to achieve. There were no references and there were no mentors.

27

After designing the games, I wanted them to be made professionally. I lived in a big city in Nigeria, so I was sure I would be able to find a company that could make the games. It was not only a frustrating endeavor, it was also unsuccessful. After a lot of walking around looking for a company, I began nurturing the idea of making my own games by myself.

Looking back now, it was one of the most daring decisions I have ever taken in my life. It is one thing to think of a tabletop game idea and maybe work on the graphic design yourself, but it is completely crazy to take on the work of manufacturing it. I am glad I made the decision! I jumped on videos online, kept practicing and seeing the possibilities. I became obsessed with boards, papers, scissors, gums, and all the other materials that I needed to make game boards and boxes and dice, too.

I didn't know it at the time, but I wasn't just making games for myself, I was building skills for a gap that existed even before I thought of my first game in 2013. I had found my purpose; I was doing what I was born to do. I was building NIBCARD Games.

In the months after my experience with the Ikorodu volunteers, I created and trained a team of young people to help me make more games. We had gotten a contract to make a couple of thousand games to help improve learning for children. It is one of the most exciting news one can get, especially at the early stage of building a company. I submitted samples of my game *Luku Luku* to the senior management team of Voluntary Service Overseas (VSO Nigeria) with a pitch of how the game will support some of the education projects targeted at children who were both in school and out of school but of school age. I remember the fears, doubts and strong hope of convincing the management that the game was a huge value addition and that we were capable of producing the games if our pitch was approved. I remember the congratulatory call telling us we had gotten the contract. I was so excited to see another potential value of games I hadn't thought of earlier – using them as tools to improve learning for children. This was what solidified NIBCARD to become a company that made tabletop games.

Spreading Influence

It is morning in Kwali, a suburb community in Abuja, the Federal Capital Territory. I am standing in front of my new home, a rented apartment that formed half of what we in Nigeria call a BQ. The sun is out but it's not too hot. There is a white plastic table in front of me full of lots of paper, strawboards, scissors, gum and dice. I am watching a video on YouTube on how to create a quad-fold board and perfecting my box-making skills. A few months earlier, I had been posted to the community to continue my volunteering role providing learning support for children who are out of school but are still of school age, mostly due to poverty or neglect by their caregivers.

We usually schedule our activities in the evening, so it makes sense to work on games in the morning. On this morning, a young boy walks up to me. I have never met him before. He gazes for a long while at the materials on the table, trying to figure out what I am doing. I notice this genuine interest from him, so I ask him his name. We chat and I answer his questions about the world of tabletop games and the game I'm making now.

It has been six years since then and that young boy is now a part of NIBCARD Games. He has also designed two very beautiful games – *Gbosi* and *Sounds Alike* – as well as other prototypes he is currently working on. I could tell similar stories of other people whom I have had the chance to talk with, answering their questions about the tabletop games industry. A lot of those people have gone on to design and publish their own games or are currently in a developing stage of their game ideas.

A Convention, a Gaming Café and More

In 2016, the same year that we established NIBCARD Games, we started the African Boardgames Convention – AB Con. At first, it was planned as an event to show more people the games I had designed but it soon grew to become a gathering of game designers, players and anyone who is interested in tabletop games from across Nigeria and all over the world. Each year since has seen new Nigerian designers, more Nigerian games, and has continued to introduce more people into the tabletop gaming industry and hobby.

This is what led to opening the first ever tabletop games café in the city of Abuja three years later. Prior to setting it up, we took games to lounges, parks and just about any space we could find, encouraging people to try games that they had probably never seen or played before. Though it was fun, it also was stressful. We then decided to crowdfund to open a safe space for tabletop gaming. It became arguably the first tabletop games café in Sub-Saharan Africa and has also become an inspiration for new cafés opening across Nigeria. The café has helped introduce more people to the industry – people whom NIBCARD Games wouldn't have been able to reach directly.

In 2021, NIBCARD Games won the Diana Jones Award for Excellence in Gaming – some other recipients of the award since its inception include Gen Con, Eric Lang, Peter Adkison, and BoardGameGeek. I remember staying up so late due to the time zone difference waiting for the winner to be announced. I was fond of the other nominees and looked up to them as well. I remember wiping the tears rolling down my face, and calling my co-founder about the announcement. Everyone was beyond excited! We had just received a global gaming award that is over two decades old, we were being recognized for what we are doing. It was a reassuring moment for all of us.

Tabletop Games Become More

I have often asked myself why I do what I do, why I became a game designer, why I started a gaming convention, why I founded a company to manufacture games, why I opened a games café, why I create regular content about tabletop games, why I resigned my job to become a full-time tabletop enthusiast in a country that has little awareness of the industry.

The truth is these are just external signs of many internal activities. I barely remember a time when I was not thinking about tabletop games or a certain aspect of the value chain of making tabletop games in the past seven years. Those moments playing with my cousins, playing in the classroom even under threat of dire consequences, when I took up the challenge of designing games with no formal background of game designs, seeing my new games for the first time – all of these moments have become the foundations of the rest of my life.

Tabletop games mean much more to me than my source of livelihood. They have become much more than a tool for people to have a great time or to improve learning or to even raise awareness on issues. It has become more than beautiful colors and folded papers. It has become more than my journey from the past or my plans for the future.

Tabletop games have become a way of life for me. And I want to live it, experience it and enjoy it every day.

KENECHUKWU "KC" OGBUAGU *is a Nigerian board game designer and founder and creative director of NIBCARD Games, a board games publisher and manufacturer based in Nigeria. He is also the organizer of AB Con, the African Boardgame Convention. NIBCARD Games was the 2021 recipient of the Diana Jones Award for Excellence in Gaming.*

MIND.
BLOWN.

John Kovalic

I remember my first Board Game as if it was yesterday.

It wasn't, of course. It was 1973, *many* yesterdays ago, and the game was *Escape from Colditz*.

I was eleven years old and my family was living in Lyddington, a tiny village in the county of Rutland,[1] in the British midlands. Oh, I'd played many board games – lowercase, you understand – before. But no actual Board Games. (Uppercase.)

There'd been board games I'd *enjoyed*, certainly: *Mouse Trap*, for example, with its sprawling, rickety, Rube Goldberg-esque central apparatus putting the "trap" into "contraption." The mechanics were rudimentary and basic (this was prior to its

---

1 Yes, as in Rutland Weekend Television. Rutland.

early revision in the early 70s courtesy of the great Sid Sackson) but the results were delightful, at least to a seven year-old.

Mostly, though, gaming to me back then had consisted of inexpensive, mass-produced trifles: hastily released lightweights, often licensing popular TV shows or movies.[2] That, or checkers with my grandfather.[3]

Cheap, licensed board games cluttered the shelves of Kmart in the late 60s and 70s, particularly around Christmastime. They were flat, rectangular boxes filled with cheap components, warped spin dials and nothing more than the most rudimentary of mechanics[4]: Parker Brothers or Milton Bradley mediocrities played with cousins, none of us expecting anything better, broken out at Christmas as soon as they were unwrapped, played once or twice, and then forgotten.

I don't remember who bought my brother and me *Escape from Colditz* when we moved back to Britain. But that changed everything, including my life.

The BBC's *Colditz* television series had proven popular – though far too tense for my eleven year-old tastes. To capitalize on its success, Gibson Games released *Escape from Colditz*, a two-to-six player game of escaping prisoners of war. *Escape From Colditz* was co-created by Major PR Reid, one of the

---

2   Remember *Dark Shadows*? The winner of the game got to wear glow-in-the-dark vampire fangs, which had probably been in at least a dozen other kids' mouths before. Forget lawn darts – it's a wonder we survived this.

3   Who wisely didn't take it easy on me. Losing a game is an important life lesson. I have lost so many games of *Munchkin*, my WIS stats must surely be off the charts by now.

4   To be fair, I may have missed some genuinely fine games in this genre. A few years ago, I played one that capitalized on the CB radio fad, named *10-4 Good Buddy*. My friend Brett's vintage copy featured *delightful* 70s illustrations and some simple yet tasty mechanics. I just ordered a used copy now, fact-checking this online. Don't tell my wife.

British prisoners who did in fact escape the "unescapable" Colditz, and named for his bestselling memoirs.[5]

The moment we opened the box and spread the board and components on the floor of our little house, I realized this was unlike any game I'd ever played before. There was the castle layout – inner courtyard, outer courtyard, surrounding grounds, tunnels, barbed wire! – overlayed by a movement grid and a series of circles that promised only this: *adventure!*

I took the role of the British Escape Officer in that first game, my brother (two years younger and easily persuaded) was left with the German Security Officer role. The game mechanics were not *Advanced Squad Leader* complicated by a long shot, but still far more involved than, say, *Monopoly, Candyland*[6] or *The Game of Life*. It took us long minutes – *minutes* – to take them all in, set up the decks and place the relevant pawns in their own particular places.

Gameplay was smooth and elegant, and eventually I had acquired enough stuff (compass, food, documents and a disguise) to allow one of my POWs to make their break!

And that's when everything changed for me.

As my prisoner of war dashed from the inner courtyard to the outer courtyard and then to the grounds, cutting wires and making good their escape, a palpable sense of excitement and danger swept over me. Every roll of the dice was critical! Each equipment card vital! I felt my pulse racing as fast as my escapee, beginning the final dash towards *freedom!*

It blew my mind.

---

5   I just ordered this, as well. Don't tell my wife.
6   It was decades later that game designer James Ernest let me in on the fact that *Candyland* is not, in fact, a game, per se. Once the deck is shuffled, that's it. Everything that follows is predetermined.

Mind. Blown.

Some forty-(mumble-mumble) years later, through a series of implausible circumstances, I find I've become a board game industry veteran (look, I *know* – I'm as shocked as anyone).

My career in games began when I was asked to illustrate the *Murphy's Rules*[7] feature for Steve Jackson Games' *Pyramid* magazine, in the mid-1990s. This led both to drawing a few cards for the *Illuminati: New World Order*[8] collectible card game (long story – don't ask) and then to Out of the Box Publishing asking me aboard their company (far shorter story – the majority owner was an *INWO* player), which soon led to *Apples to Apples*, a Once in a Lifetime Game. The INWO gig also led to Steve Jackson's *Munchkin*, a *second* Once in a Lifetime Game,[9] and this led to more than a hundred other games and game supplements for companies all over the world! I even wrote a couple, with a few more in development.

Working in the tabletop gaming biz, I've been invited to conventions across the globe, where drawing a simple Duck of Doom[10] for someone will make their day, be they from Australia, Brazil, Germany, or Italy. My comic book, *Dork Tower*, centered around a group of gamers, and eventually moved close to half a million copies over its 36-issue run.[11] Now that it's a web strip, it gets millions of page views a year. Mattel eventually bought *Apples to Apples* after Out of the Box had sold 4 million copies, and then went on to sell 16 million

---

7 A panel comic highlighting improbable or poorly written game rules. It's become an extraordinarily long-lived feature due to there being no dearth of improbable or poorly written game rules.

8 "God, I hope they don't shorten that to 'INWO,'" noted a friend, which Steve Jackson Games promptly did.

9 Math was never my strong suit.

10 Possibly *Munchkin's* most famous card. Suck it, *Dread Gazebo*!

11 Comic book creators have issues. This is well known.

more. *Munchkin* is translated into twenty other languages, and as of this writing, I've drawn nearly 8,000 cards for its many, many, *many* editions and variations. Eleven year-old me would have not known what to make of this. Sixteen year-old me would have been *bloody* impressed, though.

By the time I'd turned sixteen, we'd moved south, to Glastonbury, Somerset[12] – near my next school, Millfield. Whereas in Lyddington, I was pushing around 1:72 scale Airfix plastic soldiers (Afrika Korps versus 8th Army), in Glastonbury, my friends had purchased *actual published rules* from High Street Shops (or sometimes via mail order). These wargaming rules let you know what damage an 8th Army Infantry team would deal with their Vickers machine gun, or how fast a Panzer IV could roll, and what damage its various sides could endure. Some of my pals had painted their figures, too, with enamel paints[13] you could easily purchase in the same High Street Shops. They had rulers and dice and green felt mats for the table and... and... *everything*!

It was history come alive on a tabletop.

It blew my mind. Soon, I had both American and German forces up and running, and was slinging dice with the best of them! My tactics may have been ahistorical at best, as were some of my paint schemes (the Waffen-SS didn't go into battle dressed full in black, apparently – nobody told *me*). But

---

12 This was Glastonbury before Glastonbury really became the Glastonbury of the GLASTONBURY FESTIVAL! (Less earth-shattering but worth noting: Knight's Fish and Chips was terrific. It's still there.)

13 I didn't realize this at the time, possibly because they were all that was available, but enamel paints are terrible for painting *many* things, historical wargaming minis near the top of that list. To this day, I have whole companies of 1:300 scale micro-tanks that can be seen for miles due to their glossy, gleaming sheen.

whether it was sweeping tank battles across the Soviet steppes, or furious infantry skirmishes amongst the Normandy bocage, I was hooked.[14]

In a search of more unusual, deadlier and (frankly) cooler-looking tanks to field,[15] I'd visit Beatties model shop in Bristol (a not-too-far drive from Glastonbury), which stocked exotic treasures in 1:72 scale – Elephants and Hetzers and Sherman Calliopes (oh, my!), along with other oddities you just couldn't find in Airfix or Matchbox's ranges at the local newsagent.

On one such visit, I spotted a small stack of flat boxes on an upper shelf. Cautiously, I pulled the top one down. Its brown two-tone cover sported a Tiger tank, pointing toward me, with the bold, brash words

PANZER '44
Tactical Armored Combat
Europe, 1944–1945

In smaller type above, it noted

An Historical Simulation Game

and

The time is: 1430 hrs, 2 October, 1944

---

14 I've since revisited the rules we used back then – *Operation Warboard* and *Battles With Microtanks*. They're… essentially unreadable these days. Rules writing has gotten far better in the intervening years, as have diet soda, pub food and digital watches.

15 Some things never change.

I had no idea what it was, but I knew IT MUST BE MINE![16]
Panzer '44[17] was not a great game. But it was the first board
wargame I'd ever encountered, and yes, once more, mind =
blown.

As never before, I had entire armies at my command. Well,
companies, at any rate. OK, tiny cardboard *chits*, representing
them. The word "chit" doesn't get tossed around as much these
days. It was never as anti-cool cool as "meeple" became. Back
in the day, though, chits happened. Hundreds and hundreds
of chits, which had to be punched out, sorted and stored in
compartmentalized plastic trays. Not one of these trays ever
did the job properly, meaning that any game invariably required
re-sorting a maddening quantity of these tiny chits, which lay
jumbled and strewn at the bottom of the box, or redistributed
higgledy-piggledy among a tray's compartments, as if a tropical
storm had implausibly hit Patton's Seventh Army while
maneuvering in the middle of a German forest.[18] But reorganize
them my brother and I did, religiously, before throwing our
platoons against one another, time and time again.

It was on a trip to Bristol for another Beatties visit that I saw
something new: an actual games *store* that had recently opened!

Now, I feel it's important to point out that a games store in
the 1970s was quite different from most games stores now. It
would be decades before the large, modern, clean and brightly
lit contemporary emporiums (fun for the whole family!) began
popping up: places that *didn't* make you wonder whether

---

16 If you read *Dork Tower*, you know.
17 Published by Simulations Publications Inc (SPI).
18 If you were lucky, the games came *without* such trays, forcing you resort
    to far more reliable plastic baggies to store your chits in (or, if you were
    wealthy, *Ziploc* plastic baggies)!

someone had recently been murdered in that dark room in the back, let alone serve cappuccinos. Like ancient myriapods taking their first steps onto terra firma 420 million years ago, these initial games stores were for the most part tentative things, figuring out the lay of the land, just hoping to survive.

Across the Atlantic, Americans seemed to have had an easier time finding board wargames. Avalon Hill (initially called the Avalon Game Company) had been producing such games since 1952. Things ramped up in the 60s, and by the time I'd discovered such wares existed, you could pick them up at KB Hobby Stores in many American malls. I'd always loved visiting my grandparents in the US, and hanging out with my cousins at Johnstown, Pennsylvania's Richland Mall, but now I had another reason to cruise its gleaming collection of shiny, shiny stores.

Back in the UK, the scene was more dedicated and deliberate, but far less shiny. Long ago I forgot the name of that tiny Bristol hole-in-the-wall on its hilly street (more a sizeable cupboard with an opening onto the sidewalk, really). But it's where I discovered the Metagaming line of microgames, including *Ogre*, *G.E.V.* and *The Fantasy Trip*, designed by Steve Jackson (the American one).

It's also where I discovered *Cosmic Encounter*, the first truly *great* Board Game (upper case) I'd ever played (and the game which would later inspire Richard *Garfield's Magic: The Gathering*). Bringing new games, new *finds* to school became A Thing.

Gaming wasn't the only bond between my schoolmates and me, but it was a defining one.[19] We'd spend lunch hours playing

---

19 Along with *The Goon Show*, *The Hitchhiker's Guide to the Galaxy*, punk rock, *Monty Python* and (somewhat lower down the list) girls.

Kingmaker or *Diplomacy.*[20] Back in the States, over Christmas or summer vacations, my cousin Craig and I would pull out *Wooden Ships & Iron Men*, or *Gettysburg,* or *White Bear and Red Moon.* Later, we tried this newfangled thing that I'd stumbled across in a tiny but packed-to-the-rafters store in west London called Games Workshop. The game in the little white box was called *Dungeons & Dragons.* (It was also there, two or three years later, that I stumbled across *Traveller,* a newfangled thing that came in a little *black* box, and which would turn out to be a major reason why I flunked out of Astrophysics at Queen Mary College London, transferring to the University of Wisconsin to study Economics.[21])

Fast-forward a few decades: in my *Dork Tower* comic book, I tried to express the feeling of wonder, the feeling of *magic*, that washed over me upon entering my first proper games store.

Put simply – and you *know* what's coming here – it blew my mind.

The people behind these games – the designers, the illustrators, the artists in the credits – seemed legendary (or, at a bare minimum, impossibly clever). Dunnigan, Simonsen, Jackson, Costikyan, Gygax, Arneson, Miller, Stafford, Perrin, Pondsmith, Jaquays… these were giants, to me. That several of them later became good friends or colleagues or both still gives me pause.

---

20 If you've ever played *Diplomacy*, it may come as a shock to you to learn that we're all still friends.

21 Econ came so easily to me I could skip two out of three classes and still earn straight As. This fit well with my gaming schedule.

I turned sixty last year.[22] I've been a gamer for forty-nine years, if we're going to count *Escape from Colditz* as my gateway. It was re-released a couple of years ago by Osprey Games, and darned

---

22 Which strikes me as ridiculous, at best, and implausible, at the very least.

if it didn't give me the chills, opening the new box, and seeing that familiar map: Inner Courtyard, Outer Courtyard, all those rooms, the trails one had to dash, the barbed wire.

The history of board games stretches back millennia, starting (as far as we know) with the Royal Game of Ur, and almost certainly quite a bit earlier than that. The last fifty years have been a period of unprecedented growth and innovation in the hobby, with constant change and occasional upheaval in the business. It's been wondrous to watch, and equally amazing to have been a tiny part of it for nigh on thirty years now.

On one level or another, the greatest friends of my life have all been gamers, be they the school chums I played *Kingmaker* with, the college mates I'd stay up all night dogfighting in *Air War*, the industry pals I look forward to hanging out with at conventions, or the best friend I've ever known, my wife, who bought her wedding dress with money she made from selling a *Magic: The Gathering* Black Lotus card.[23]

And now, my wife, our kid and I will spend evenings after supper, playing games like *Above and Below*, *Bad Beets*, *Dragonwood*, *Go Nuts For Donuts* and so, so many others.

The change in the board gaming hobby since the 70s has been seismic, but one aspect, for me, at any rate, remains the same.

Several years ago, I was sitting on a motel floor, in the Bay Area, with a few of the good folks from GeekDad. I was there with them for the Maker Faire, where they had a booth.

Jonathan Liu, their resident board game expert, had just laid out the tiles and cards for a new game he'd come across, called *Forbidden Island*. The rules for this Matt Leacock classic

---

23 Yes, yes, yes – I know it's worth a lot more now than it was twenty-five years ago. But the story alone is worth it.

Mind. Blown.

cooperative game were elegant and accessible,[24] and quickly we were in a critical race to shore up sinking tiles,[25] combing the doomed isle, trying desperately to collect the artifacts we needed before screaming precariously to the helipad, hoping we had the requisite cards needed to fly us to safety.

I honestly don't remember if we won or lost that first game. But I do remember the clear, palpable feelings of excitement, danger and jeopardy the game created, and the laughter and the shrieks as chunk after chunk of the island sunk, and the cheers as an artifact was saved that punctuated the warm summer night.

This game, like that very first board gaming experience a lifetime earlier... worlds apart. But entirely similar.

They both blew my mind.

Board Games (uppercase) probably always will.

JOHN KOVALIC *is a cartoonist, illustrator and games designer who has designed or illustrated games including* Munchkin, Whad'Ya Know, *and* Apples to Apples. *As a cartoonist, he is best known for his* Dork Tower *comic and as an award-winning editorial cartoonist for the* Wisconsin State Journal. *His work has also appeared in the* New York Times *and* Washington Post.

John's Dork Tower *comic strip is published at dorktower.com*

---

24 If you think board games have come a long way, rules writing has come even further!

25 Who names areas "Cliffs of Abandon" or "Dunes of Deception"? *You had one job,* Island Chamber of Commerce!

THE LONG GAME

Christopher John Eggett

When I was nine years old, I walked into my Nan's kitchen and saw, on the purple carpet-tiled wall, a hand-drawn poster on cheap, thin paper. It proclaimed a contest would be held, and that I was to take part. There was a date for the bout: today. My competitor would be my great grandfather, who went by the nickname of Grag. That's how he'd written it, too, "Christopher vs Grag."

The game was one I was familiar with. Dots would be scattered in a grid across a piece of paper. We would take turns joining one dot to another, attempting to create closed-off squares. Each square would be filled with the competitor's initial, a C or a G, and each was worth a point. The real battle was to try and snooker the other player into taking a smaller slice of the area – and giving up the rest for you. Taking the last move for just the right number of points to come out on top always felt like such a sweet victory.

We knew this game as dots and lines, and, for me, there's no way of thinking about it without it triggering the memory of this time and place. The game was first published by French mathematician Édouard Lucas, but to me it feels like a game that simply existed from a time before I could remember anything.

If you ask most people about board games, they'll give you a story about a place, a time, a person they played with. Even if that's just *Monopoly* on Christmas Day. Games punctuate our lives and our memories because of the magic that happens when we play them. They set out a particular way of interacting with other people that asks you to put aside the "real" world for a moment and engage with people only within the arena set out by the game and its rules.

Games are the perfect objects for connecting moments and parts of our lives. You can look at your life and tell the story of how you became the person you are today through the games you were playing at the time. This isn't to say that the games you play make you who you are, but that the games you enjoy reflect your experience of life of the time. Looking over our own collection is a way into plotting out our own autobiography through games, and when we look at what hit home with us the hardest it's sometime something inherent in the kind of play they produce that makes them valuable to us.

My father died on September 29, 2005, when I was eighteen. He was forty-five. My brother was fifteen. I'll spare you the details of a tragedy. In the year of mourning that followed my brother and I spent a great deal of time playing a lot of PlayStation 2 games in companionable almost-silence. It was a ritual for us to sit in the end room at our Nan's house playing slightly old games, just being there with one another. That time we spent being present for each other was important to us as, even though much of what we felt could not be articulated, we knew for sure that we were the only ones who understood. In the years that followed this closeness began to dissipate as we were forced to get on with having lives.

It was only years later, when I broke out *War Chest*, an abstract game of asymmetrical warfare, with my brother that I realized how important that time had been. In *War Chest*, there's a back and forth between players as you attempt to gain control of a majority of the scoring hexes. *War Chest* asks you to draft a set of poker-style pieces with individual movements and attacks, like archers who can shoot over other units, crossbows who shoot straight across and cavalry that can only attack in a charge. Only one side will have access to a particular unit type, so your choice is important. In repeated games this drafting becomes an important metagame. For me, this mirrored the specific kind of "competition as an excuse to be present for one another" that was helpful as young men who can't articulate their feelings of grief fully. Those repeated plays ended up being a moment of reconciliation with that shared grief. In the game you end up playing not against a person and a board state, but against your unspoken understanding of them.

Before this, the first game that really got me into "proper" games was *Carcassonne*. When my friends and I were in our early twenties, a group of us would usually book a holiday cottage somewhere in the depths of the British countryside and go race our bikes up and down local hills. We'd go away for New Year's Eve and cook huge amounts of food. One year we brought *Carcassonne* with us. I could argue that a game about building a little world together (or against one another) in the idyllic landscape mirrored what we were doing in our real lives – making attempts to map the world out, trying to build up as much as we could in our name, occasionally ruining one another's day. But it's more about how this game existed in this particular group of friends. You see, we owned it as a group. Each trip away, we would add another expansion to the set. It became a wandering ronin of a game, living in various members of the group's houses until the next time we were all together again – this time adding the (quite silly) The Princess & The Dragon expansion (when a dragon tile is drawn, it goes for a wander and eats meeples, everyone gets a turn moving it) or The Tower (where you can attempt to build towers and kidnap other players' meeples, charging a ransom for their release). This ritual of sharing and expansion was an expression of our friendship and a realization that these were people we all trusted implicitly and without thinking.

Another game that reflects something back about the stage of life I was at when I came across it is *Oath*. When my daughter was a few weeks old, I spoke to Cole Werhle, the game's designer. *Oath: Chronicles of Empire and Exile* is a game about endless legacy. Many legacy games involve irrecoverably changing the game – often by applying stickers to the board or ripping up cards. *Oath* isn't like that. In *Oath*, each faction within the game has cards removed or added depending on their performance, changing the mix for the next session. Equally, the locations that are being fought over remain between sessions and if the regime is overturned (for it is a game about revolution) that location is cast out into the hinterlands and new ones are drawn. The spark that this game grew from, according to Cole, is playing old Avalon Hill games procured from secondhand shops with missing pieces, the wrong rules, or an unmentioned expansion mixed in. The idea was that these games developed their own kind of play that was unique to each box's available or unavailable parts. There's a magic in the idea that a game has been touched by someone and passed on, changed.

When I was speaking to Cole about this, my daughter was around twelve weeks old, and like any new father, I'd decided a couple of things. One, that I would live forever if I had to if it was to her benefit and, two, I wanted to scoop up as much as possible of the world that existed before she was able to remember things and save it for her. It's a funny old thing becoming a parent. When *Oath* finally arrived a year and a half later, I realized it was just what I needed for the second of those decisions. Each play of the game subtly changes the board state and the cards available to players the next time round. *Oath* rewards players for taking actions that affect the world – and any grand plans mean nothing if they don't make a difference to how the board looks when you put it away, saved for the next game.

For example, if someone negotiates a non-aggression treaty with another player – something that happens naturally over the table during the game – and then turns on them to take the win alone, the game's landscape and mechanics change with the way they've exerted power. If someone decides to take the offer of citizenship (a way of sort-of winning the game with the current regime) those choices are recorded in the changed world. The game records their actions a little like the real world does – as in, the ones that make an impact are the ones that are remembered. And here – in my game of *Oath* – everyone who touches the game leaves their mark on it, too. I imagine, maybe a little romantically, that I could one day pass this game on to my daughter, and it will contain a little bit of the time that someone spent with me playing this game through the impact they had on the world that was packed away in the box. These might be people who are no longer with us or those who we've just lost touch, but their actions in the game affecting the actions of those who play next, and beyond that. It's a folly to think you can really pass anything on like this – but it's the kind of thinking you end up with once you have a child.

Oath started out as the game that was going to be a project for my daughter to carry on, but I think, in truth, looking back three years later, there are much more likely candidates.

During the lockdowns in the UK, we weren't able to meet up in person. Our group (the same one that, ten years earlier, had been throwing ourselves up and down hills on bikes between games of *Carcassonne*) played games online. It started with sessions of *Mörk Borg* and ramped up to *Alien: The Roleplaying Game*. The games we played reflected our need to be doing something important at the start of the lockdown. It felt like everyone was struck by a kind of ennui, and moving from a silly death-metal game to the more complicated and narratively tight *Alien* felt like an upgrade on doing nothing. But then we hit an almost-violent tiredness of communicating through screens. The most we could now manage were little games of *Wavelength* – a perfectly fun (and easily videocalled) game of guessing how others think on a scale of this to that. You ask people to rate something from superhero to supervillain, and you guess where that rating is on the scale – and then you argue about it afterward. These games show how we moved from trying to have a big entertainment experience through to just trying to find a connection with others at all. As the pressure of that time increased, we searched for meaning in the microscopic elements of our lives while ignoring that which loomed so large. If the life-through-screens hell of the lockdown period was akin to endless small talk, then *Wavelength* is a perfect engine for generating the better kind of idle prattle.

If I was going to predict the future and guess which game would be the one that I associate with the next stage of my life, it would come back to my daughter. Sometimes we play "the fighting mouse game," or as it's also known, *Mausritter*. *Mausritter* is a roleplaying game about adventuring mice in a world of honey-addicted cultists, sunken temples, and paw-friendly arcane magic. It runs on Into the Odd as a system, and the combat can be brutal, as you'd expect for a mouse using a needle as a rapier. And she loves it. She comes up with solutions to problems I wouldn't have thought a three-and-a-bit year-old could possibly come up with. She's learned that even if the dice don't go her way, the story is always interesting. I'm just hoping she'll still be interested in making up things with her dad when she's old enough to want to play a full campaign. As much as *Oath* felt like a game that reflected me becoming a father, it's going to be a game like *Mausritter* that'll actually belong to her. The lesson is probably something about understanding that you don't get to tell your children's stories. We can help to tell the beginning, but we can't say how it's going to turn out.

So, then, it's time to cast an eye at your own collection and look to find the games that you've played at the highs and the lows in your own life. The games you keep for sentimental reasons, and perhaps chide yourself for. Look at them again and find how they tell the story of your own life. Because this is why games matter – it's not whether I won a game of dots and lines thirty years ago, but why we were playing at all.

CHRISTOPHER JOHN EGGETT *is a writer and game designer from Cambridgeshire, UK. He was previously the editor of* Tabletop Gaming *magazine and now runs Ada Press Games with his partner where they make "stupid little games."*

You can find Christopher at www.cjeggett.co.uk

VICTORY POINTS, REP, LABOR & DELIVERY

Cathleen Williams

"I am *not* going to the hospital tonight!" I growled at Daniel, my husband, as he entered the bathroom in the middle of a deep contraction, hoping to convince me to do precisely that.

I am ready to deliver any moment. This will be baby number six. At this point in motherhood, I claim to have the divine power to choose a birthdate for my daughter with more auspicious lotto-winning numbers than today. Everything else is ready: my parents are watching our older kids, my favorite things and necessities are packed – the warm cozy socks, a cute postpartum outfit, skin care, lip crème, charger, cellphone. However, this time around, I have stuffed a special treat in my suitcase – a copy of *Palm Island*, a simple game about village building with just seventeen plastic cards – portable, sanitizable, and no table required.

As a mother of six children under the age of ten, my days are action-packed. How do I have time for board games? Like they say about hitting the gym, "You make time for it." I accompany my evening tea with therapeutic card-sleeving and meditative component-counting. I went on a decade-long, love-hate hiatus from tabletop gaming after my parents left seven year-old me to play *Mastermind* and *Guess Who?* alone. College was all about party games like *Pictionary*, *Cranium*, Texas hold 'em – conventional fun. It was after marriage that my cardboard gaming passion was revived with dear, sweet *CATAN*.

And then… my family continued to grow! Any hobby is a source of guilty pleasure when you must tend to children. So, I broke up with board games again and ended up drowning in parenting shoulds and should-nots. My mental health spiraled, and my therapist suggested taking up a hobby. What I needed was something I enjoyed prior to marriage and that I could involve my family in. This phenomenal panacea, *tabletop gaming!*

The benefits continue to amaze me: the development of patience, concentration, communication and critical thinking skills, tricking the kids into doing math, and an incentive to tidy around the house in order to find some delightful gaming time. It is my first-choice method for making like-minded friends – crucial to an isolated stay-at-home parent.

Flashforward. It's about 7:30 PM, and I have sworn to myself to not birth this child until after midnight when it will finally be the eleventh day of the eleventh month – which sounded cool to me. "Bring it, baby! Mama has got this!" I scoff, recalling my last labor experience when I had time to give myself a gel manicure and pedicure between the paralysis-inducing contractions. I was fantasizing about my hospital stay and planning the ultimate guilt-free, couch-potato board gaming binge. I enjoy my haughty fortitude for another two minutes until the next contraction obliterates it. Launching from my bed to the passenger's seat, I yell for Daniel to grab the luggage and to teleport me to the delivery room.

Forty-five minutes later, my newborn daughter is warming my clammy arms. I'm drained from the pain, the pushing, the crushing of poor Daniel's hand. My hunger gives me a spike of energy, enough to devour a sandwich. After a brief nap and getting a sense for the flow of doctor and nurse visits, I sneak a game in of *Palm Island*. By round two, a doctor is checking up on me and a nurse hands me my medication. Attempt one is foiled. While breastfeeding, I start a game of *Ticket to Ride* on BoardGameArena on my mobile phone. My railroads are going cross-country, until I wake up to a red notification, telling me I've been expelled from the game after I fell asleep with –10 percent reputation! The BGA system doesn't hand out "free to be a jerk" cards to new moms, and rightly so.

That wouldn't be the only time I lost reputation during my hospital stay. A healthcare provider checked on me and I forgot I was mid-game. Disappointed by the loss of my reputation points, my eyes were glued to my cell phone screen when the next physician came in. Now I was being awkward in real life, and compromising my health for fun's sake. Sleep deprivation scrambled my priorities. I grudgingly made it through a single game of *Palm Island* to complete my personal objective before the hospital registrar came to document my newborn's birth. Again, my heart was torn – I hadn't prepared a name for her! Then it hit me – this is precious one-on-one time with our new addition. Babies grow and change so fast and I need to be fully present for her. The board games can wait for a bit.

I can't recommend gaming at the hospital for first-time moms or casual gamers. Aside from it being a turning point in your life, it also isn't exactly a walk in the park. But for those who, like me, really can't do without, I did learn that digital board game apps and online board game sites are much more accessible than physical board games at the hospital. Phones and tablets are easier to sanitize than meeples or cardboard tokens any day. Another lesson is that it is poor etiquette to waste other players' time just because you are sleepy or get distracted. Playing against the computer or a solo game are better alternatives.

Our games don't have to collect dust – better if they don't. Like they say, "Happy parent, happy house." I've learned that balance and self-care are key to being a good parent and, for me, that means making time to play games with my family and friends. I have a weekly group for heavier weight games, weekends are set for family gaming, and once the kids are in bed, I get online for BGA. Good luck and have fun, gamer parents!

CATHLEEN WILLIAMS *is a medical laboratory scientist turned stay-at-home-parent and playtester from Seattle, Washington. When she isn't tabletop gaming, Cathleen can be found hanging out with her husband and seven children, enjoying a game of golf, indulging in neon-colored cotton candy flavored ice cream, and pampering the hummingbirds in her garden. Her gaming mantra is a quote from George Bernard Shaw – "We don't stop playing because we grow old; we grow old because we stop playing."*

GAMES
ARE LIFE

Matt Forbeck

The way Dani Rojas feels about soccer on the Apple+ TV show
Ted Lasso is pretty much how I feel about games. When we first
meet him in the show's first season, Dani is a fresh-faced recruit
to the team, and he's a ridiculously positive and happy player
whose catchphrase is "Football is life!"

I'm a lot older than Dani and have been at my particular
passion for much longer, but I feel much the same way. To me,
"Games are life!"

Let me explain.

I've been playing games of one sort or another since before I
can remember, whether that was peek-a-boo or tag or war or any
of the other forms of child's play that many of us grow up with,
horsing around with family and friends. The first time I actually
remember playing a game, though, was when I was six years old.

I was a sickly kid. I had terrible asthma, essentially from birth, that kept me from doing all sorts of things, although not for lack of trying. This was before we had decent medications for asthma, and I wound up visiting the emergency room in my local hospital – often multiple times a week – for years. It got so that my parents and I knew all of the doctors and nurses there by name, and they would all stop by to say hi when I was in.

The routine was pretty much the same every time. They'd get me registered at the front desk, then set me up in a room with a nasal cannula that provided me with the extra oxygen I needed while I was wheezing in as much air as I could manage. I can still remember the plasticky smell of those transparent tubes and the cool feel of the oxygen flowing across my upper lip on its way into my nose.

After that, the doctors and nurses would inject me with epinephrine (a synthetic adrenaline) in one arm and wait to see what happened. This is the same stuff you find in an EpiPen these days, but back then they didn't have autoinjectors. And no one trusted a young kid to run around with a pocket full of syringe-accessible glass bottles and the hypodermic needles necessary to draw the stuff out and stab it in.

Well, rightly so.

I don't know if you've ever had a shot of epinephrine, but it works a lot like the adrenaline your body produces when you've had a close brush with death, or at least a terrible fright. It gets your heart pounding, wakes you right up like you're never going to sleep again, and – most importantly – opens up the bronchial tubes in your lungs so you can get as much precious oxygen into your bloodstream as you're going to need to deal with whatever triggered that reaction. It can take a while to come down from it and get your heartbeat back to where it should rightly be.

It was rare that a single shot would be enough to handle a serious asthma attack, though, and they often had to give me more. For that, they would just move over to my other arm and jab me there, and if that didn't work, they'd proceed to my legs. They just kept rotating through my limbs until I started breathing easy again, which could take a couple of hours or more. After all of that, they'd give me a shot of something similar but with a longer half-life and send me home, hoping not to see me again – or at least not soon.

Life went on like that until I was nine years old, at which point a number of amazing new medications came out that substantially cut down the time I spent in the ER. These treatments have gotten so good over the years that these days I barely ever have to use a rescue inhaler at all, and I haven't been rushed into an ER for an asthma attack since I was in high school.

So in the end, it worked out pretty well, and it also made me a huge believer in medical science. If not for that amazing but steady progress, I'd have died long ago, I'm sure, and I do my best to make the most of all these extra years.

The low point in my struggles with asthma came when I was six years old, back around 1974 or '75. I had what we'd all thought was a pretty bad cold with a wet, hacking cough, and when I started having trouble breathing, my parents drove me to the emergency room, like always. After shooting up every one of my limbs with adrenaline at least twice, the doctors sent me for a chest x-ray. When they brought the films back to my room and took a look at them on one of those wall-mounted light boxes, they discovered that I had developed what appeared to be a gray fog inside my lungs.

The diagnosis was bacterial pneumonia. With asthma like mine, that was a dangerous thing to have.

The doctors admitted me into the hospital proper for a

longer stay, and I soon found myself in a room in the children's ward. Instead of using a cannula to help me breathe, they put me in an oxygen tent. This is a pup-tent-sized structure made with clear plastic walls that sits over your entire body while you lie in bed, with the exceptions of an opening at the top (where the air could flow out) and one at the far end (where I could stick out my feet).

I remember the oxygen tent being incredibly humid. Condensation got on everything.

I was a big reader, even at six. I spent countless hours sitting in my school library in the early parts of asthma attacks, reading while I waited for my mom or dad to get free so one of them could pick me up and bring me to the ER. A local reporter even spotted me there as he wandered through the school one day, and he took a photo that wound up in our small-town Wisconsin newspaper.

This was in the days before home video games existed, much less early handheld rigs like the Nintendo Game Boy. Phones weren't even portable then, much less smart. Because of my health, I spent a lot of time sitting and waiting, and not having access to such modern conveniences, I learned to always bring a book or three with me everywhere I went.

While I was stuck in the hospital for a whole two weeks, I found a pile of comic books about a foot high in the playroom they had on the children's wing, and I read through every one of them. When I was done, my parents supplemented that with a fresh stack of comic books they'd bought for me. I kept them beside me in the bed, and the humidity from the tent warped every last one of them.

Even with all that reading on hand – plus loads of regular books to boot – I got bored. I loved having people visit, but they weren't allowed to be there for too long and never overnight. That was the first stretch of my life where I remember sleeping alone, not at home in the room I shared with my younger brother.

So, I was thrilled when our family priest showed up to visit. I was raised Catholic and would start attending Catholic school the next year, in second grade. My parents had both gone to similar schools and then met at Marquette University, a Catholic college. In those days, they were solid members of our local church, which had two priests – an older pastor and a younger associate, Father Steve Zwettler.

Father Steve, as we all called him, wasn't all that far out of college himself. My parents would invite him over sometimes for dinner or to watch Marquette basketball games on TV. My dad liked to curse loudly when watching games – a habit I may have inherited – but he did his best to curtail that when Father Steve was around. He wasn't always all that successful at censoring himself, but my siblings and I thought it was absolutely hilarious to listen to him try.

After I'd missed Sunday mass due to being detained in that oxygen tent, Father Steve came to visit me in the hospital. While he was there, he asked if he could give me Last Rites.

As you might imagine, I found that a little disconcerting, but Father Steve quickly explained to me that I wasn't about to die – at least as far as he knew. The sacrament commonly known as Last Rites is properly called the Sacrament of Extreme Unction. "Unction" just means to anoint someone with oil, which he would apply to my forehead with his thumb as he prayed over me.

It's the "extreme" part that's unsettling, of course, as the sacrament is only meant to be given to people who are extremely sick, perhaps in danger of death.

Trusting in Father Steve, I clung to that "perhaps" pretty hard. I'd been hacking up my lungs for over a week at that point, and I was starting to wonder if that might be the start of a slide that would wind up with me living in a plastic bubble for the foreseeable future.

Father Steve explained that, while he was no doctor, he understood this to be very unlikely. He simply wanted to perform Extreme Unction for me as a precaution, to make sure that if something happened, I'd head off to heaven with a clean slate – and to maybe help give me a fighting chance.

Maybe that wasn't the best way to try to set a six year-old's mind at ease, but I trusted his judgment and agreed to go along with it. Afterward, he followed up the Last Rites with something that made me think he really did believe that I was going to make it.

Father Steve had brought a chess set with him.

He showed it to me and asked if I wanted to learn how to play. I'd heard about the game but never actually tried it, and I instantly said yes. He opened up the box, laid out the board, and set up the pieces on the side of my bed, where I could reach it by lifting up the edge of my oxygen tent.

That game hooked me good.

He patiently taught me how the game worked, focusing on how – unlike in most games I'd enjoyed to that point – each of the types of pieces had its own way of moving and its own role to play in the match.

The idea that games could work like that surprised me. The shoe in *Monopoly*, for instance, doesn't work any differently to the top hat or the dog. They just mark a player's position on the board. In chess, though, you marshal a whole team of pieces, many of which have wildly different ways of moving around the board and capturing or cornering your opponent's pieces.

We played multiple matches before it was time for Father Steve to leave. When my parents next came by, I told them all about it, and not long after that I had a new chess set of my own to play with. It was one of the classic teaching sets with the moves for each piece diagrammed out on the side facing its player.

I wound up playing my parents countless times with that set and even roping in my siblings as they got older. Beyond that, though, it opened up the world of games to me, not just that of the old classics but that of new games you could play in all sorts of different ways.

From there I moved into other games like *Stratego* and *Risk*, and countless more that are now new classics in their own rights.

One summer while I was in high school, I tried my hand at starting my own tabletop gaming magazine – *The Quill & Scroll* – which published a whole two issues before finally folding. That cost me my life's savings at the time, of about a thousand dollars, but I never regretted spending a penny of it.

Setting that up with my pals, writing and editing the articles, lining up ads and subscriptions, working with printers, distributors and stores – every bit of that taught me far more about how publishing works than any class I ever took in college. That summer, we even had our own booth at Gen Con – the biggest tabletop games convention in the world – and I met so many people and made so many friends that it helped launch me into a career as a game designer and a writer.

As I write this, I've had more games and books published than I care to count, over a professional career that's already lasted more than thirty years. I've created board games, miniatures games, collectible card games and roleplaying games, and I've worked on several video games as well, from *Assassin's Creed: Origins* to *Biomutant*. On top of all that, I've had somewhere north of thirty-five novels published, most of them based upon games.

I've been to Gen Con every year that it's been held since 1982. I've been freelancing for the tabletop games industry since I was in college. I co-founded a game publisher – Pinnacle Entertainment Group – and served as its president for four years before I went back to freelancing. (I love playing games and designing them. Selling them? Not nearly as much.)

My latest tabletop game is the *Marvel Multiverse Role-Playing Game*, which will be out before you read this. It's been a pretty good run for a kid whose family priest gave him Last Rites at six years old.

The most important thing that Father Steve did for me, though, wasn't to perform that sacrament. It wasn't even that he taught me a new game. It's that he taught me the game when I was that close to dying. That – more than anything else he could have said – told me that I was going to be fine.

You don't teach a dying kid a challenging game that can take a lifetime to master. Not if you really think they don't have much time left. That comforted me a lot more back then than any prayer – and I think it still does.

After all, "Games are life!"

MATT FORBECK *is an award-winning and* New York Times-*bestselling author and game designer with over thirty-five novels and countless games published to date. His projects have won a Peabody Award, a Scribe Award, and numerous ENNIEs and Origins Awards. He is also the president of the Diana Jones Award Foundation, which celebrates excellence in gaming. He is the father of five, including a set of quadruplets.*

You can find Matt at forbeck.com

PEOPLE

FRIEND IN A BOX

Gav Thorpe

The Early Years

Like most folks, my earliest gaming recollections are of playing with family. We were quite a gaming family, I suppose. We had all the usual family games such as *Frustration*, *Mouse Trap*, *Operation*, and the obligatory compendium of chess, draughts, Chinese checkers and backgammon. I recall a *Buckaroo* clone based on *Jaws*, with a rubber band-powered shark mouth to pull things from. This was atmospherically more frightening but lacked the sheer explosive power of a plastic mule shedding its load. Other classics like *The Game of Life* and *Alley Cats* expanded the collection and later more adult games such as *Monopoly*, *Cluedo* and *Trivial Pursuit*. We sometimes played card games like Newmarket or Hearts on a Saturday evening before bedtime.

There were also games on the shelf that were not the norm, at least as far as I was aware at the time. My brother had an early polyomino placement game called *Skirrid* that set us up to be *Tetris* addicts later in life. A strategic game with a Napoleonic theme called *Campaign* sat alongside *The Business Game* (AKA *Mine a Million*), which allowed us to create our own industrial empires. A particularly noisy favorite was *Sonic UFO*. Of course, there was also *Electronic Battleships*. British folks recollect the frustration of trying to load a ZX Spectrum game from tape and having it fail after five minutes, but that paled in comparison to ten minutes of carefully entering coordinates into *Electronic Battleships* only for it not to give the ready tone, indicating a mistake had been made somewhere along the way and a full reset was needed. From such ordeals were a generation of coders born.

Into my teens these family games swelled with acquisitions like *Scruples* and *Dare*, and only recently my dad reminded us of the Saturday afternoon we spent inventing a game to decide which game to play, which took so long there was no time to play the game we decided upon.

However, by then something else had happened to dictate the future course of my life...

At Easter time, to ensure that we weren't overly burdened with chocolate eggs, my grandparents used to give my brother and me presents instead. One set of grandparents gave us Lego, the other gave us games. Sometime around the age of nine or ten we received a couple of games that were a bit different. One year it was a very strange game called *Dungeons & Dragons* – but that's a story for a different book. Another time it was two boxed games, one about dueling wizards called *Warlock* and the other called *Valley of the Four Winds*. These were early Games Workshop board games and I suspect the choice was somewhat influenced by my older cousin, who was into fantasy in a big way, and my main guide into the world of miniatures and roleplaying.

Having been introduced to the concept of what we might now call hobby games, I was hooked. Most notable over the coming years would be *Talisman* and its many supplements. My brother and I would play weeks-long games over the summer holidays, maxing out our characters, using only the Horrible Black Void, Demon Lord and Dragon King in place of the Crown of Command to ensure the experience wouldn't end too soon. My hex-and-counter games collection expanded with the addition of *Goblin*, for which my dad kindly mounted the board on a piece of 2' x 3' hardboard, and so it has remained to this day through numerous house moves!

Top 5 Games Most Ten Year-Olds in 1984 Didn't Play

1 *Warlock*
2 *Valley of the Four Winds*
3 *Magic Realm*
4 *Goblin*
5 *Attack of the Mutants*[1]

The Awkward Teens

Rick Priestley, creator of *Warhammer*, once described a game as "a friend in a box." Many of us will recognize the slightly uncharitable truth of this. Socially a bit awkward, into geeky stuff in the 80s and 90s, games were a bridge between me and other people. This manifested in three ways.

Firstly, there was solo gaming. I spent hours playing alone. Games like *Icebergs*, *Chainsaw Warrior*, and the wargames from

---

1 Much to my irritation, this is the only one on the list I don't still have.

Battle Games Book 4: World War II. I began to realize that I liked all kinds of games that let us tell stories. Arnold Rimmer's *Risk* diary[2] may be as dry as the Sahara, but the actual highs and lows, the surprise successes and the near misses are something a game gives us to talk about years later. At least, if the game is any good.

This leads me to the second tranche of games that came to dominate my tween and teen years – Games Workshop. By now they had pivoted to being the *Warhammer* company, mainly focused on miniature battle games. But that didn't stop them bringing out some cracking board games. For a start there was the *Wargames* series of *Battle for Armageddon*, *Horus Heresy*, and *Doom of the Eldar*. I played these with my gaming buddy Danny. Danny was the friend I played miniatures games with, and all things *Warhammer*ish. I have a vague recollection that I became friends with Danny because I happened to spot a doodle he had done on a school notebook – something to do with another classic GW board game, *Space Hulk*. Having found a fellow gamer, the brakes came off the miniatures side of things.

Thirdly, as well as introducing me to Danny, *Space Hulk* being not as scary as a *Warhammer* army or as nerdy as a hex-and-counters game served as my "geek test" game for other potential friends. There were a couple of kids at school that showed some interest after playing *Space Hulk*, but our friendships never progressed from there. On the flip side, my good friend John, with whom I mostly played on his Spectrum and later his Atari ST, was a fan of the US National Football League (as was I), newly arrived to UK television. Naturally,

---

2 In TV sci-fi comedy Red Dwarf, Arnold Rimmer has a campaign diary of every game of *Risk* he's ever played, but it is basically a list of moves and dice rolls without context – "So a six and a three and he came back with a three and a two."

I recruited him to second edition *Blood Bowl*, which was mainly played when he came to my house (as I lacked the aforementioned Atari ST, though I had inherited his Spectrum +2).

Even as the allure of beer and single malt whisky grew more prominent, the games were still there. As we hit the age when we could reliably get served in a pub, John and I would meet up with another friend, Lee. The three of us would crash at Lee's (parents') place, listen to Pink Floyd and Fleetwood Mac, while the two of us would drunkenly play chess. A couple of times all three of us tried to play *Risk*, but after awakening too many times to a mess of pieces and scattered cards, we soon gave up.

After finishing sixth form, John, Lee and Danny headed off to respective universities across the UK, leaving me alone in the cultural dry ditch that was Stevenage New Town. Its saving grace was a great hobby stall in the indoor market that later became an actual store, and a comics shop that stocked RPGs. Gaming went back to solo mode but was about to change my life forever.

Each of those games had planted a seed in me, and having decided against a career as an illustrator, I thought about various gaming-related jobs I might do. This included, at the unlikely age of eighteen, opening a model shop! Having some experience as a Dungeon Master and gamemaster, and after tinkering with rules and a bit of fiction writing for fun, I wrote some extra rules for *Blood Bowl*. For those interested, they introduced quadrupeds like Zoats and Bull Centaurs (being a grid game, these rectangular-based pieces needed a subset of special rules). In 1993, Danny and I met up for our twice-yearly pilgrimage to Games Day (or perhaps it was Golden Demon), a gaming convention organized by Games Workshop. It was here that I presented my efforts to the esteemed Jervis

Johnson, designer of *Blood Bowl*, to ask him what he thought. He glanced at them, said they looked interesting, and then uttered the fateful words, "Don't give them to me now, I'll lose them. Send them to me at the Design Studio."

I looked up the address in *White Dwarf* magazine, typed up a cover letter on my mum's electric typewriter asking if they had any vacancies, and gathered together some other bits and bobs I'd worked on. The rest, as they say, is history.

Top 5 Games I Wanted as a Youth but Never Had

1   *Car Wars/Battlecars*
2   *Hedgehogs' Revenge*
3   *Atmosfear*
4   *Stratego*
5   *Curse of the Mummy's Tomb*

The Euro Invasion

As you might expect, my first couple of years at Games Workshop were dominated by miniatures games. However, as I moved from assistant games developer to *White Dwarf* staff writer, I came into the circle of newly minted editor Jake Thornton. Jake was another polygamer and it was through him that my gaming world would again explode, much as it did when I received that copy of *Valley of the Four Winds*. Jake, you see, was near the frontline of a wave of games crossing from Germany into the UK, different from the hardcore hex-and-counters and family games we'd been used to.

Jake was my gateway into the eurogame.

I suspect that many folks reading this are of similar vintage and experience of the 90s gaming boom. This was when *Settlers of Catan* arrived, and a host of German games were being translated into English. Quite often Jake would only have the original game in German, with a self-printed version of an English translation from some new-fangled thing called the World Wide Web. We played *Modern Art, Mississippi Queen,* and *Pico* alongside Avalon Hill classics like *Squad Leader* and (as far as I was concerned at the time) unknown games like *Nuclear War* and various Cheapass Games' titles. *Ra, Tigris and Euphrates, Bohnanza, Nicht de Bohne,* and *Guillotine* hit the table, and it was at this time I met Max and Simon, GW colleagues from outside the game design department, with whom I became very good friends. As well as the collective gaming sessions, Simon and I branched out into hex madness like *Dragon's Pass,* and a couple of brain-taxing sessions of *Statis Pro Football* (being NFL fans). The group went separate ways eventually under the general momentum of life and geography as I neared my thirties, but there was one true heart that remained.

Top 5 Games from the Early Euro Arrivals

1   *Settlers of Catan*
2   *Durch die Wüste* (*Through the Desert*)
3   *Mississippi Rose*
4   *Carcassonne*
5   *Modern Art*

The Middle Ages

In terms of longevity and most number of games played, my most consistent gamer friend has been Max. As I type this, we're due to get together in a few days, more than twenty-five years after those first games of *Bohnanza* and *Kill Doctor Lucky.* There have been times of plenty when we gamed every week, but there have also been some leaner times – even before the pandemic, growing families and the whole life thing put a huge spanner in the gaming works.

Eclecticism has been the theme of our gaming relationship, with an obvious slant towards two-player games, but there are a few that we come back to again and again. First and foremost are the Columbia Games blockfests, with *Hammer of the Scots* (about which I wrote an essay for Green Ronin Games' *Top 100: Hobby Games*), *Rommel in the DesertI*, and *EastFront: The War in Russia 1941–1945* topping the bill.

Later on, heading toward my thirtieth birthday, I formed a poker-playing group that evolved into a more general board games night. Regulars were Matt, Andy and Erik, and through this group I was able to enjoy some of the bigger games out there like *Battlestar Galactica*, *Chaos in the Old World* and *Pandemic*. To this day I have not forgiven Andy for throwing me in the brig as a suspected Cylon, even though I was president, and despite it being obvious that Erik was almost certainly the traitor within! This group also allowed me to indulge in my secondary gaming hobby – backing games on Kickstarter. A slew of Tiny Epic games ensued, and *Cthulhu Wars*, *The Faceless*, along with *Who Goes There?* (based on the novella that became *The Thing*) which enabled Andy to reprise his role as inadvertent turncoat.

My Kickstarter habit subsequently escalated to a frankly unhealthy degree on the justification that I would play them with this group. Of course, the group has scaled down to three of us meeting maybe once a month if we're lucky, but those KS projects from two years ago keep arriving...

Top 5 Games I Play(ed) with Max

1   *Hammer of the Scots*
2   *Commands and Colors: Ancients*
3   *Hera and Zeus*
4   *Star Wars: The Queen's Gambit*
5   *Twilight Struggle*

Fatherhood

As I entered my fourth decade of existence, a new one came into being in the form of my son, Sammy, marking this latest and most significant stage of my gaming life. His mother is, of course, a gamer too. Before his arrival, and for a year or so after, we would enjoy a seven-hour session of *Sid Meier's Civilization*, or a long visit to the Dice Cup board games café learning *Stone Age* or *La Granja* (wife Kez is a fan of engine builders and worker placement). Nowadays we're fortunate if we get in a quick game of *Patchwork* or *Azul*, and often resort to a game of *Dobble* (*Spot It!*) when we're out for a coffee just to keep the dream alive. If we get someone to babysit, we often go back for a heady couple of hours at one of the local board games cafés.

But with that lack of time for one sort of gaming has come plenty of time for another sort. We are raising Sammy in the true geek way, and that includes making the most of the gamer gene he has clearly inherited. We've never wanted to create negative associations with books or games, so from toddler age onward have allowed him to (carefully) look at games, play with the pieces, and one of my favorite photos is of him sitting proudly next to the map he constructed from *CATAN* hexes. Orchard Games formed a big part of his infancy, and as his reading and numeracy skills in particular have come along fantastically, games with more complex rules have followed.

These days, to be a gamer parent is to live in a golden age. Although there's still suffering through Snakes and Ladders, explaining (again) why *Monopoly* isn't all that fun *even with the Star Wars* pieces, there are so many good games produced for kids and parents, or that are suitable in general. Co-op games neatly avoid the need to "let the Wookiee win" to avoid tantrums from an overtired seven year-old, so *Forbidden Island* has featured quite frequently. A cousin of his mother is an avid gamer and has supplied him with suitable gaming presents for several years, including award winners like *Ghost Fightin' Treasure Hunters*, while acquisitions like *Zombie Kids* and *Kraken Attack* are perfect. Even on the more competitive side there's the joy of *Rhino Hero* (or more specifically *Rhino Hero Super Battle*), because even if he loses, he gets to see those card buildings tumbling down.

Sammy has turned nine now, and continues to develop his own preferences and strengths. As well as classics from my own childhood like *Escape from Atlantis, Eye of the Idol,* and *Lost Valley of the Dinosaurs* (for which he created a surprisingly workable co-op version recently) he's just beaten me at a game of *Space Hulk* (how the wheel turns) and forced me to accept his rule with *Conquest of the Empire*. He hasn't quite got the Pokémon bug, much to his mother's disappointment, but the arrival last Christmas and birthday of the CMON *Mayhem* games for Teen Titans and Looney Tunes proved an instant hit. The joy of poring over the map in *MicroMacro* or flicking penguins around in *Ice Cool* is just as fun for an adult as it is a child, while *CoraQuest* is doing an admirable job of staging the way for some *Warhammer Quest* or similar in the next year or two.

For myself, the biggest development has been to acknowledge the same truth that existed when I was thirteen and setting up another *Winter War* by myself: my hunger for games outstrips the people I have to play them with. So, somewhat encouraged by a worldwide pandemic, my solo collection has made some decent progress. Notables include the *Great Sieges* series by Worthington (though actually they work better as two-player games, I have discovered) along with some of their other titles such as *Keep Up The Fire* and *Tarawa, 1941*. A gem I discovered on Kickstarter is a roll-and-write game called *USS Laffey – the Ship That Would Not Die*. Others that have found their way from pledge to shelf are *Ratcatcher* and *Veilwraith*; as with many things, the pandemic-powered surge in solo gaming has seen a likewise increase in great titles to collect. With these I have been able to get a gaming fix even when the rest of the world has been unavailable.

So, after all this, perhaps my most important gaming buddy has always been my imagination.

Top 5 Games Most Nine Year-Olds in 2023 Haven't Played

1   *Hera and Zeus*
2   *Conquest of the Empire*
3   *1565, St Elmo's Pay*[3]
4   *Forbidden Island*
5   *Space Hulk*

GAV THORPE *is a British writer, games developer and creative consultant. In the world of games, Gav is best known for his work on the* Warhammer *series of games and worlds. As a writer, he is a New York Times-bestselling author, and winner of the 2017 David Gemmell Legend Award for Best Fantasy Novel.*

You can find Gav at gavthorpe.co.uk

---

3   Technically I was playing this solo, but Sammy was picking and playing cards for the other side.

HOW TO TALK TO THE PEOPLE YOU LOVE, STEP ONE

Gabriela Santiago

As my half-brother turned ten, I noticed distressing signs that he was becoming a jock.

Granted, if he was becoming a jock, he was doing so in the nerdiest way possible. He memorized statistics: RBI, field goal percentages, touchdowns. Much in the same way that, as a toddler, he had watched the weather channel and tracked weather patterns, he now tracked the scores of baseball and football games. Because I lived in Minnesota, the Minnesota Vikings were "your Vikings," and he would tell me how they were doing on every visit I made to their home in Illinois, with the stats to back it up.

My half-sister was not yet a jock – she was still reliable for a game of "Cats." This was a game where we both pretended to be cats and had entire conversations in meows as we tossed cat toys back and forth. I was very good at it. In time, she too would display an unnerving degree of physical coordination that would lead her to the basketball court and a record-breaking performance on the track team.

I was then a self-described nerd in my early twenties, and was, naively, scared of what it would mean for our relationship if we had such different interests. This is the thing about family that we are not shown on TV. Yes, you love them, but love is not the same as understanding, and it is possible for the people you love to become strangers. If I had still lived in Illinois, my siblings and I might have grown and changed alongside each other, which would naturally have been less alarming. But I had stayed in Minnesota after college, had found a city that I loved and wasn't ready to stop exploring, and so, though I had fond memories of the corn and soybean fields, I had no intention of going back.

When my siblings were very young, before I left for college, we had played board games every time I visited – my dad or my stepmom would suggest them after supper was cleared away, sending my little brother or sister to the old toy room to haul out battered boxes of *Trivial Pursuit* and *Pictionary* and *Uno* and *Telestrations*, or brand new ones purchased seemingly just for this occasion like *Jenga Quake*, a new version of *Jenga* where the blocks were slippery plastic and the base on which the tower was built randomly shook and buzzed, guaranteeing that no game lasted longer than a couple of minutes.

But now, suddenly, things were hard. Conversations got more stilted. My siblings are over a decade younger than me – we were watching different TV shows, reading different books.

They were teenagers navigating all the intricacies of middle and high school, and I lived so far away from that experience, farther away than merely miles and years.

Visiting Aledo, Illinois, I struggled for words, heard my voice crack. When I was back in Saint Paul, Minnesota, I mailed letters with candy and stories enclosed. The subtext beneath every one was *see me love me see me respond*. I found myself not inhabiting the role of older sister, but auditioning for it, desperate to get it right.

It seems like such a simple thing, being able to talk with your family. But for the first twenty years of my life, I'd been baffled at how some interactions rolled along without a hitch, while others stalled in silence. I was in college before the revelation struck me like lightning that *I could ask questions*, even if I wasn't intrinsically interested in the thing I was asking questions about, because the thing I was most fundamentally interested in was the people I was talking to.

Even after this revelation, it was still hard sometimes to talk to my siblings, to honor the people they were becoming when so much of my brain was lit up with fear that I was losing the people they had been before. Fear is the grit that catches in the wheels of social interaction, slowing and stalling and sometimes breaking the thing you are trying to create.

As I felt the distance grow, I decided to lean into the family tradition of playing games. A game is a useful contraption for structuring a conversation. Instead of flailing about for topics, they are provided along with the board and dice. What will we talk about? We will talk about the game. We will review the rules, we will choose our game pieces and our partners. "I was the shoe last time, I want to be the cannon this time." "Do we have a dictionary? I think we should allow proper nouns too." "I want to be on your team."

In the course of a normal conversation, it can be hard to really listen to each other. So much of the time, there are anxious bees circling inside your skull. It can feel like a volleyball game, waiting for it to be your turn to respond, worrying that you might lose if you don't return the serve. Think of something interesting, think of something witty, think of something genuine and heartfelt! Think of it quickly, before the moment passes you by! But the board game takes away the pressure. You respond in the moment honestly and concretely. Without the need to come up with these things on our own, we can relax, take a deep breath, and make our next move. "Uh ... Borneo?" "In what way was that supposed to be a dog?!" "I'm going to let you take this one."

Before you know it, you're laughing together, at your dad's attempt to draw a gorilla or at someone's choice to pull the worst possible *Jenga* tile. You're discovering – or rediscovering – one person's silly victory dance, another person's inability to not talk through the other's turn. Oh, here is my brother, of course he got that answer about sports right, of course he didn't know the one about Star Trek, that one was for me. Oh, here is my sister, here is the face she makes when she sees my description of my dad's drawing and has to draw something in return. We begin to defer to each other's specialties, or rib each other gently for our shortcomings.

We begin to realize that we are family, and around a table where a board game is laid out, we can get to know each other again.

Covid made things harder, because of course it did. My family aren't Covid deniers or anti-vaxxers by any measure – my dad and my stepmom are both doctors – but their risk assessment is different than mine. By the time I finally felt safe enough to take a plane again, they had been attending baseball games and eating in restaurants for months. Days before we were supposed to meet up, I was testing negative every twenty-four hours but had a bit of a sore throat and a cough, and I agonized over whether I should still go. They invited me to a White Sox game.

It's hard living in a different world than the people you love. I ended up visiting them at their house, but I wore a mask the entire time. I don't have the sensory issues with masks that some people do, but when you're already batting below a hundred (did I use that sports metaphor right? Another thing to ask my brother) it's another impediment to communication. Your eyes have to do so much more work to show that you are smiling, your voice has to do so much more work to tell people you really are happy to see them.

I thought I was probably safe. But what if I wasn't? What if I took off my mask and killed the people I loved?

The car ride was stilted, me trying to think of things to ask, the conversation petering out after a few sentences until someone tried to resuscitate it.

But then we got to the house, and we brought out the games.

Place card box, sand timer, clean-up cloths, and die in center of the group.

If the player has no matches or they choose not to play any of their cards even though they might have a match, they must draw a card from the Draw pile.

Roll the die to decide who goes first. Highest number rolled takes the first turn. Play continues clockwise.

This is how we say, "Hello. I love you. It's so good to see you again."

We're taught that family is instinctive, but it's not always. Rules change. The scripts that we followed at one age no longer make sense, and we have to write new ones. As we grow, we take on different roles, where we're needed for fewer and different things. It's how it goes.

But in a game: here are the rules. It will be your turn, and then it will be mine. Here is a list of choices you can make. When I win, I say something goofy like, "Bow before me!" When you win, you do that little smirk, the one that looks a little like mine. Around and around the table we go.

It's okay for it not to be instinctive. It's okay to need an assist sometimes.

Nothing fixes everything, at least not forever. We're alive, and therefore so are our relationships. I haven't seen my siblings in person since that last covid trip. In the course of writing this, I was texting them about the games we had played together, and I realized we had never played *CATAN*. Do you know what a travesty that is? I rule at *CATAN*.

We're definitely playing it next time I'm in town.

GABRIELA SANTIAGO *is a graduate of the Clarion writing workshop and a member of SFWA. Her fiction has been published in venues such as* Clarkesworld, Strange Horizons *and* The Dark.

You can find Gabriela at gabriela-santiago.com

BOARD GAMES EQUAL FAMILY TIME

Will McDermott

I grew up playing games. All kinds of games. At our house we played board games, card games and eventually (for me at least) roleplaying games. From an early age, I equated games with family together time. Later in life, I transferred this together time to my friends and my own family. It was a time to socialize and have fun being together.

I remember lazy Sunday afternoons playing cribbage and backgammon with my mom and dad. I also played both of these with my best friend on long afternoons after school. I still have the cribbage board and the backgammon set my parents gave me some fifty years ago as birthday or Christmas presents. I taught my son to play cribbage on that same board, and I have wonderful memories of playing with him in airports while waiting for connections (even after we gave him a Game Boy).

Back in the day, before the advent of handheld games, my family took decks of cards, my cribbage board, a backgammon set, and the vinyl, fold-up *Tripoley* game mat on vacations. I absolutely loved going fishing with my family while growing up. Fishing was the together-time my dad had with his father as a kid, and he wanted to share that experience with his sons. Ironically, it was always my mom who caught the biggest fish. After a long day of fishing, all we had was each other, a table, and a deck of cards. I loved those vacations, but I remember playing games at night and on rainy days just as much as I remember the fish we caught.

My brothers and I also have fond memories of playing board games with our cousins every time we went to family reunions. We played classic games like *Candyland* and *Mousetrap*, although we never actually played *Mousetrap*. We just set it up and tried to catch the mouse. As we got older, we leveled up to the likes of *Monopoly*, *Life*, *Careers* and *Risk*, which we played late into the night. In retrospect, these games were there to keep us kids quiet for hours, but it worked, and we forged long-lasting bonds with our cousins that continue to this day.

College Days

As I became geekier and nerdier (mostly from hanging out with my *Dungeons & Dragons* group), I found European-style strategy games, which took playing board games to a whole new level. I first got hooked in college on the likes of *Civilization* and *Gammarauders*, and later played *Settlers of Catan*, *TransAmerica*, *Carcassonne*, and *Formula Dé*. These games really made you think while playing, though, so sometimes the social aspect of playing them took a back seat to the competitive nature of the games – and the players.

I remember one session of *Gammarauders* with a bunch of college gaming friends where I got incredibly upset with the game, and my friends. *Gammarauders* is a silly game of powering up weird kaiju animals with crazy, oversized weapons and crushing your opponents (and the city). The problem was that the rules as written allowed for ganging up on the current leader at the end of the game, so it could easily get to a point where the game could literally never end. After several cycles of this happening during one session, the game became un-fun for me. That was the first time I ever rage-quit.

That night of *Gammarauders* might be the moment I realized that I like games for the camaraderie more than the competition, even though I am often the most competitive player at the table. It also was a turning point of sorts in my life, and not just in my game-playing habits. At first, I tried to craft some house rules that would "fix" the game. This was somewhat successful and led me further down the path toward becoming a game designer.

Adults Play Games, Too

My introduction to the game industry came when I landed the job of Senior Editor on *Duelist* magazine, the original magazine about Wizards of the Coast's *Magic: The Gathering* game. Producing a monthly magazine is a lot like a complex cooperative game. The editors must work together with freelance writers to produce all the copy needed for each issue. Then the editors cooperate with the graphic designers to produce the final pages of each issue. Once each issue is complete, you get to start all over again. I loved it. Every month we got to work together to create a new, shiny product together.

It was hard work, but it was the best time of my life.

We, the editors and designers, also played together outside of work hours. My wife and I hosted board game parties like our parents used to host cocktail parties. Our game days, however, were way more focused on playing games and eating than hanging around together to drink and complain about work. Don't get me wrong, we complained about work and had a beer or two, but the focus was on playing games, having fun together and building rapport as a team, which we then brought with us back to the office.

Game days became such a thing in our lives that the idea of going to a party and not playing games seemed foreign. We have friends from that time who held an annual game convention in their home. People signed up for games, brought food for the entire group and just hung out for as much time over the course of a weekend as they wanted, playing games and enjoying each other's company.

Another friend still has an annual New Year's Eve board game party that's been happening for decades. Some of the friends we see there we don't see the rest of the year, so it's a great time to get together, play some new games people have discovered in the past year, and ring in the new year in the company of old friends doing the thing we all love the most – playing games.

Board game parties are way more fun than cocktail parties. At a cocktail party, the only activities are drinking, snacking, and talking. To me that's kind of boring. People tend to gather into small groups to talk about themselves or the people in the other groups. Sometimes there are activities, but you know what? Those activities are, more often than not, games. Think about it. Charades, *Pictionary* and any number of party games have been created to add some life to dull cocktail parties.

Instead, why not just invite people over to play board games for a night or for a Saturday hang-out day, or maybe even an entire weekend for a miniature game convention? For me, bringing people together to share a fun experience of playing board games while eating food that is bad for you is a much better experience than breaking into small groups to gripe about work and talk about people who annoy you. My wife started planning such a weekend event for my next birthday, which is a major milestone number. I can't wait to turn sixty now!

The Joy of Cooperative Play

I absolutely love cooperative games. The first of these games I ever came across is one no one has ever heard of: *Minion Hunter* by GDW, made as a simplified version of their *Dark Conspiracy* RPG. My wife and I won a copy of this game at a GAMA convention decades ago and have played it at least a hundred times over the years with friends and our kids. In the game, you try to improve your character along the outer, *Monopoly*-style track so you can battle demons on the US map dominating the center of the board. It takes careful coordination and some amount of luck to beat the game and is a hell of a lot of fun.

Since *Minion Hunter*, we have collected a lot of cooperative games. Our favorites are *Pandemic, Sentinels of the Multiverse, Arkham Horror,* and *Horrified,* which sets the group against the classic monsters of old movies.

A subset of cooperative games are asymmetric board games, which pit one player against the rest of the group. The first of these my wife and I ever found and fell in love with was *Scotland Yard,* in which one player is "Mister X," and the rest are members of Scotland Yard trying to track the nefarious criminal through the streets of London. It's a blast to play and, again, requires plenty of good, old-fashioned teamwork to beat Mister X.

In the end, the team aspect of both cooperative and asymmetrical board games is what appeals to me the most. I played organized baseball growing up and have always been a fan of watching team sports. I love team sports because good teams are built on the camaraderie between players working together toward a common cause. That's probably why I also love the TV show *Ted Lasso*, and what drew me into playing roleplaying games in college.

I enjoy learning new games with friends and family because this experience can be cooperative even when playing a competitive game. Playing a new game for the first time with friends who already know the game is actually a very cooperative task. Plus, there is very little pressure to perform well. It's a new game to you, so you expect the person teaching you to understand it better and do well. For me, anyway, this helps curb my competitive side, which allows me to enjoy the experience of learning the game even more.

Sharing a game you truly love with a friend or family member also makes for a great bonding experience. You get a chance to enter the world of the game your friend or loved one enjoys and see why that game appeals to them, which can bring you closer as you play. You also get some insight into a person's psyche by seeing what types of games they like to play, which can help your relationship, and maybe even teach you something about yourself.

For example, I have plenty of highly strategic friends (and two strategic, intelligent sons) who absolutely love resource management games like *Alien Frontiers*, *Lords of Waterdeep* and *Terraforming Mars*. I enjoy some of these and will play them, but after a lifetime of managing people and processes on tight deadlines, those games don't appeal to me as much anymore.

Family Games

Game vacations can be an amazing experience to share with a geeky family. As our kids grew up, our vacations centered around game conventions. We went to Gen Con, PAX, Origins, and small, local conventions with our kids in tow. There we played games, visited with old friends from the game industry, and enjoyed the camaraderie of gathering around a game board to move meeples around and roll a bunch of dice.

Playing games as a family makes for a wonderful, shared time where everyone can have fun doing a common activity. In today's world filled with devices that promote solo activities, getting the entire family to sit down at the table to play together is a great way to reconnect with everyone after a long week of work and school. It's a time to relax, enjoy each other's company, and come together as a family for a night.

My kids are grown and out of the house now, but we still get together once a month or so to play games for a day. Games have always been our family time together, and that hasn't changed now that they are adults with their own lives. And, when we spend that time playing a cooperative or asynchronous game, the experience brings us closer together because we are all working toward a common goal.

Today, my wife works for Funko Games, a wonderful board game studio in Seattle. Every month, her office holds a game night at the studio, complete with pizza and drinks. Everyone brings in their favorite new games to show off to others and share the joy of the game. I look forward to this night every month because I get to play new games and reconnect with people I have worked with on other projects.

Games are a great way to blow off steam after work and share a connection outside the stress of the workday with coworkers, friends and family. Funko Games encourages spouses and children of employees to attend, showing that the higher-ups understand the value of play for the morale of their employees (which is rare, even in the game industry, from my experience).

A Lifetime of Games

So, what have I learned from a lifetime filled with board games? Well, first and foremost, board games are a great way to bring a family together over a shared experience. You don't need any special abilities to play games other than the appropriate age to understand the rules, so it's an activity that is open to all.

Unless you are super-competitive and are having a rough run of luck where you keep losing every game, playing games with friends is a purely positive experience that brings people joy and provides a light, inviting atmosphere for building friendships that will last much longer than the memory of any single game you won, lost, or even rage quit. I am still good friends with that *Gammarauders* group from my college days. We just don't play that game anymore.

I wouldn't change the role that games have played in my life for anything. Games, for me, were and always will be the best time spent with family, friends, and even coworkers.

WILL McDERMOTT *has published nine novels and twenty short stories, often set in gaming universes including* Magic: The Gathering, Warhammer 40,000, Renegade Legion *and* Mage Wars. *Will has written for* Choose Your Own Adventure, War with the Evil Power Master, ESPN Trivia Night, The Goonies: Never Say Die *board game, and* Cranium 25th Anniversary Edition *for Funko Games.*

You can find Will at willmcdermott.com

BONDING OVER BOARD GAMES

Sen-Foong Lim

It should be obvious to anyone who is even just starting to get into the hobby that people play games for a lot of different reasons. So, it would stand to reason that people design them for a lot of different reasons as well, right? While some people start designing games because they have a great idea that they need to get out of their head, others are trying to turn their hobby into a job. Still others are looking to get their name on a box.

Me? I just wanted to stay in touch with my best friend.

Jay and I both went to school at McMaster University in Hamilton, Ontario, Canada in the early 90s. Jay and his housemates were hosting a house party and our mutual friend, Errol, had invited me to tag along. Errol and I walked across campus one hot and humid summer evening and made our way to the party, guided there by the siren song of loud music and rowdy laughter. We made our way through all the people and Errol introduced me to Jay, who was, at the time, standing in the driveway. Without skipping a beat, Jay smiled and asked, "Do you want to see my Amiga?" It was as if he sensed that we were kindred spirits, like I set off his nerd-radar or something. And really, what self-respecting video gamer wouldn't want to see Delphine Software's *Out of This World*[1] running on Commodore's then state-of-the-art sound and graphics powerhouse? Of course I wanted to see his Amiga!

Over the next few years, Jay and I bonded over a mutual love of all things geeky: movies, comics, tv shows and – of course – games. Games have always been a huge part of my life. I had cut my teeth on traditional roleplaying games as a young boy in the late 1970s, learning to play *Dungeons & Dragons* in the appropriately dungeon-like basement of Algoma University in Sault Ste Marie. My frustrated mother carted me off there when, as a precocious six year-old, I had read both *The Hobbit* and *The Lord of the Rings* and devoured all of the fantasy novels my local library had to offer. I instantly fell in love with roleplaying and enjoyed the hobby all throughout elementary school and high school. Some might say that I enjoyed it too much. Instead of mathematical equations, any graph paper I got my hands on became a dungeon. Any school project I did was immediately focused on mythology or turned into a game somehow. As the kind of student who passed classes with flying colors despite being focused on imaginary worlds, this all backfired severely when I got to McMaster and found out that university-level courses required actual effort to pass! So, I did the most mature thing I think I've ever done – I went on a self-imposed moratorium from playing *D&D*

---

1   Known as *Another World* outside of North America.

and other tabletop roleplaying games. It was that or fail out of school. As the son of Chinese immigrants, the second option was unacceptable, so I went through the difficult process of weaning myself off my childhood passion.

Being the 90s, however, *Magic: The Gathering* quickly filled the hole in my heart left by RPGs. Both Jay and I were instantly captivated – it's called "cardboard crack" for good reason! More than just playing the game incessantly, we began to think about *Magic's* design. If Helen was the face that launched a thousand ships, *Magic: The Gathering* was the game that launched a thousand fledgling game designers down that career path. So many of our current colleagues are past Pro Tour players or designers from Wizards of the Coast. From a design standpoint, Magic was so eye-opening because the core conceit of the game at the time was that there was a metagame in which you built decks between playing the actual game, and in putting a competitive deck together, you were learning the intricacies of the game itself. Each deck was a little game design exercise in and of itself! We spent many an hour building decks, testing and retesting them. I was even a member of many Usenet groups, at the dawn of the internet, that centered around designing mock cards. Dissecting single cards to see what made them tick became a nightly activity. Eventually, the constant urge to collect took its toll on us. It wasn't healthy for our meager wallets and so we stopped playing after the *Ice Age* expansion set was released in 1995. It was as if that set had cooled our passion for the game, though not for gaming.

I found some solace in *Warhammer 40,000*, another game I loved but could not continue to justify the expense. Eventually, I completely gave up on both *Magic* and 40K, selling my prodigious amounts of cards and minis to fund my postgraduate degree. They were just too much of a time sink for me as I was starting to get serious about my future. While neither were as all-encompassing as RPGs used to be, they still occupied much more of the brain space that I needed to reserve for my studies. Jay had moved on from these lifestyle games as well and went to work for what would eventually become Best Buy Canada. Thankfully, Errol (always trying to introduce us to fun things) taught us a game he had learned to play with his church group – *Settlers of Catan*. And with that, we found our niche. The influx of so-called "German Games" in the 90s allowed us to have our cake and eat it too. We could scratch that itch for playing a game with meaningful decisions and put it back in the box and on the shelf until the next game day. Board gaming wasn't like *Magic* where we were constantly building new decks, nor like 40K where we were desperately (and poorly) painting miniatures to field. It was much less demanding on our limited time and resources. It was perfect. So, we dove into board gaming headfirst and didn't come up for air until the new millennium.

The year 2000 was a pretty big deal for me. A lot happened. I graduated and started my clinical practice as a pediatric therapist, married Carrie (the love of my life), and we purchased a cute little hundred year-old house at the ridge of the escarpment together. I needed somewhere to put all of the board games I had accumulated, after all! It was then that Jay and I really started to work on designing games. We'd meet at my house after work and on weekends to play games with funny German names like *Bohnanza*, *Adel Verpflichtet*, and *Ursuppe* while dreaming of making our own. An idea formed in our heads, and we put pen to paper, merging tile-laying, exploration, and *Indiana Jones* – Jay's favorite movie franchise. Jay had the idea of making a game where there was a hidden treasure, but its location would have to be different every time since the map was generated through play. We thought that using landmarks and piecing together a treasure map would allow us to accomplish this lofty goal. Enthusiastically, we made a prototype, played it, made changes, and played it some more. We did this over and over for a few months, but we couldn't make it work. It just wasn't fun.

We failed.

So, we packed the game away and with that, we thought our dreams of becoming game designers like Klaus Teuber, Sid Sackson, Alex Randolph, or Reiner Knizia had gone up in smoke. We didn't stop playing games, but we gave up on designing our own, resigned to the fact that we just couldn't make one worth playing at that time. Our love for games didn't die, but our passion for design was snuffed out with that single negative experience.

Over the next few years, both Jay and I experienced some major life changes. While I had suffered quite serious injuries from a near-fatal car accident, Carrie and I also had the joy of bringing our first child, Ethan, into the world in 2003. Jay, on the other hand, moved from the shop floor to corporate HQ doing product training for salespeople. This necessitated a cross-country move from Ontario to British Columbia. For those readers not familiar with Canadian geography, that's over 3,300 km away as the crow flies (about 2,000 miles) and three hours of time difference. So, now, not only were we failures at designing games, but we were also unable to play games together, period. Our shared hobby was no more.

We both played games with other people, of course, but it wasn't the same. We didn't grow apart, but our friendship was getting more and more difficult to maintain. We were moving in different directions and in different social circles. I was solidifying my chosen profession and growing my family back in Ontario while Jay was exploring new places and spaces and meeting new people on the west coast.

Right before Ethan turned two years old, we took him to Vancouver to meet his Uncle Jay for the first time. During this trip, Jay and I, of course, played many board games and our passion for design was rekindled. We made a pact right then and there to once again make a concerted effort to design a board game. Really, it was a method of maintaining our long-distance relationship. Though playing games across the internet was clumsy at best in the early 2000s, designing them proved to be much easier, at least from an infrastructure standpoint. As I had been very active on internet forums at the turn of the century for my music-related hobbies, I knew that we could use one to house our design documents and keep track of our projects. The asynchronous nature and organizational structure of a forum allowed us to work collaboratively while in different time zones. Being three hours ahead of Jay, I would go to bed after writing him a note about a game we were working on and wake up to feedback on that note. We'd go back and forth in this somewhat slow but steady fashion. I personally think that co-designing across a large distance really forced us to hone our communication skills, support our ideas with evidence through testing, and articulate the ideas we were *really* trying to convey to each other.

Working remotely had its downsides, of course. We couldn't test games together so we wouldn't have the same experiences. We'd have to make multiple prototypes, which could get onerous for games that used highly specific components like Junk Art. It was even difficult to schedule meetings with publishers where everyone was available at the same time. Thinking back, it's amazing that we got all of that work done across such a great divide!

Like any meaningful relationship, we've had our ups and downs. We've had to work things out, mostly because of the differences in our life stages – not because of game design conflicts. Carrie and I had a second son, Elijah, in 2008, and moved to London, Ontario, a year later to be closer to Carrie's parents. Jay didn't have children until 2017, but when he did, he went all out and had twin boys. I can't even imagine all the diapers that Harrison and Everson produced at once! Earlier on, I just couldn't be as productive as I had other roles and responsibilities I had to prioritize at that time and, similarly, Jay's life got *much* more interesting with the birth of the twins! Each time there was a problem, it took open and honest communication to get past the hurdle. We've had to grow as friends and partners as we've expanded our range to include not only games that we've designed, but also games that we do the art direction on and games that Jay publishes through his Off the Page Games imprint. As the stakes increase, so does the risk and the reward.

Though we mostly see each other in person at conventions, we are still there for each other when life throws us a curveball, whether personal or professional. When one of our games gets dropped from a publisher's roster or a publisher terminates a project that we were excited to work on, we call each other. It helps to have a partner who knows, intimately, what it took to get that game designed and published. It makes the lows not so low. Conversely, it makes the highs all the more high! Having a friend to share the accolades and recognition with makes it so much better. While we appreciate each of our games, our two favorites aren't necessarily the most loved because of how successful they were financially. *Akrotiri* has a special place in our hearts because it took the novel procedurally generated map idea from our failed first prototype and turned what was merely an okay game into a game loved by two-player game aficionados around the world. *Mind MGMT* is our more recent favorite because it not only allowed us to work with one of our favorite comic book creators, Matt Kindt, but it was the first game Jay ever released. We were recently recognized outside of the hobby gaming industry for Mind MGMT with a nomination for a Harvey Award in 2022 in the category of Best Comic Book or Graphic Novel Adaptation. We lost to the Disney+ series, *Ms Marvel* – we were punching just a wee bit above our weight class, so we were just astounded to have been nominated!

Thirty-two years on, despite the distance and the differences in our lives, Jay and I are still the very best of friends. We're like most other friends except that we create games together. As we grow older, our lives continue to be centered around games but our friendship extends well past gaming. Our daily chats almost invariably turn to our families or Brazilian jiu-jitsu (a martial art we both practice along with our kids) while we're planning our next release or discussing a new idea for a game, but we're also there for each other when things are rough. When my father was diagnosed with dementia, Jay was one of the first people I talked to. When Jay's father passed away, I was one of the first people Jay called. We're friends first, co-designers second.

As Off the Page Games grows and as I'm thinking about retirement from academia, both Jay and I are beginning to realize that there are other possible futures for us in gaming. Will I continue to co-host the *Ludology* podcast and the *Meeple Syrup Show* or will I join Jay at Off the Page Games? Will Jay leave Best Buy to continue to write books in his *Fail Faster* series that teaches people how to design games or will he focus on being a publisher? Who knows what the future will hold.

The only thing I *do* know is that Jay and I will always remain the very best of friends.

All because of games.

SEN-FOONG LIM *is the co-designer of board games like* Belfort, Akrotiri, Junk Art, Scooby-Doo: Escape from the Haunted Manor, *and* Mind MGMT: The Psychic Espionage "Game" *with Jay Cormier, as well as* The Legend of Korra: Pro Bending Arena, *and* Kingdom Rush: Rift in Time. *He has also co-authored several RPGs, including* Jiangshi: Blood in the Banquet Hall. *Sen co-hosts the* Ludology Podcast *and the* Meeple Syrup Show.

You can find Sen at senfoonglim.carrd.co

THE GAMER GENE

James Wallis

The history of board games in Britain is a long and illustrious one. From the Lewis chessmen (actually, they're probably Norse, and chess is from India), to the nine men's morris boards carved into the cloister seats of most of our medieval cathedrals, we are a nation of games-players hooked on games made by people in other countries. The first properly British game is *A Journey Through Europe or the Play of Geography*, a simple race game by John Jeffreys, printed in London in 1759. It created an explosion of British games in the late eighteenth century, designed to educate the children of the newly wealthy middle classes in how great the British Empire was. Most of them were simple roll-and-move games, beautifully illustrated but not very good by modern standards. One of the main publishers of these, responsible for over forty titles between

1790 and 1847 – including *Every Man To His Station, The Mirror of Truth* and *The New Game of Human Life* – was the London-based father-and-son firm of John and Edward Wallis.

Scoot your eyes back a page to remind yourself of my name.

I'm not a direct descendent of John and Edward, but they're in my family tree. At the time they were designing games at 42 Skinner Street, Snow Hill (next door to another children's publisher at 41, one William Godwin and his daughter Mary, who would shortly run away with Percy Shelley, write *Frankenstein* and invent science fiction), there was an extended Wallis clan printing and engraving all manner of things across the capital. My branch were mostly making engravings of landscape pictures by famous artists, notably Turner.

I learned about John and Edward in 1998. That was five years after my first card game had come out, and I'd been running the largest roleplaying game publisher in the UK for almost half a decade. It seems unlikely that there's a genetic base for a predisposition towards game design or games publishing, but if anyone wants to do a case study then I'm probably patient zero.

Given all this, it's hardly surprising that I seem to have slid from game designer to game historian, delving into the sadly neglected history of the field. This also means I can expand my collection with many delightful oddities, while fending off any thoughts about pruning it back: "No, I still need that, it's for research."

Like a lot of gaming parents, I have tried to pass on my passion to my children, with variable success. The youngest is now a firm *D&D* player, which brings joy to my heart, except that she refuses to play with her *paterfamilias*, preferring to campaign with a group of friends from school in a homebrew background so creatively weird that in the near future I may be making them an offer to publish it.

As for my oldest, she's at an age where sport and social activities are more interesting than anything her dear papa could suggest, though it wasn't always that way. I run a workshop, a crash course in tabletop game design called the Game Design Masterclass, in games stores and cafés up and down the country, which has given me the privilege of introducing several thousand people to the art and science of making board games.

A few years ago, I ran a session of the Masterclass for grown-ups at a games café in a hipsterish area of London, and took my eldest and her friend Thomas along, it being the summer holidays and my turn for childcare. They enjoyed themselves during the talky bit, but when we got to the actual making-stuff part of the workshop, where the participants divide into teams, invent and build a game, and then playtest it with the other teams, I asked if any of the teams would be willing to include the kids, but the young professionals declined. To be fair, they were paying to be there, and it was perhaps a bit much to expect them to entertain two excited ten year-olds at the same time. Anyway, the kids were happy enough on their own and quickly got absorbed in their own design.

I always give the teams a theme to use as a jumping-off point for their game ideas, something that can be taken in many different directions, and this time it was simply "London." They rose to the occasion, producing a diverse range of games with different mechanics and surprising complexity, given the very short time they'd had. One thing that there's never enough time to cover is for every team to play all the other games, so as part of the final wrap-up I ran through what each group had produced:

"Team A and B have both done games about commuting on the tube, but came at it from different angles, one about trying to get a seat and the other about keeping your stress level down. Team C has a game about setting up a chain of coffee shops, and Team D has created a race to be the first to take snapshots of different tourist attractions around town. Great work, everyone, give yourselves a round of applause." I paused. "Meanwhile, the ten year-olds made a game where you play a refugee who's fled their country with nothing, and you have to survive living on the streets."

The Game Design Masterclass isn't a competition. It's not about designing the best game, it's about learning the process of creation and iteration, and how to collaborate and share ideas. But from their faces, I could tell the grown-ups knew they'd been outplayed.

Games are for everyone. Anybody can design a game about anything, in an hour, with just paper and pencils, and that's a powerful thing. And whether or not there's any genetic basis to game-design talent, I think John and Edward Wallis would agree, and they would be proud of how far we've come, and where we're going.

JAMES WALLIS *is an award-winning games designer and author. As a designer, he is best known for* Once Upon a Time *and* The Extraordinary Adventures of Baron Munchausen. *His books include* Everybody Wins: Four Decades of the Greatest Board Games Ever Made *and* Board Games in 100 Moves *(with Sir Ian Livingstone). He lives in London with his wife and 1D4-1 children.*

More information on James's Game Design Masterclass can be found at gamedesignmasterclass.com

PLACES

POLAR BEAR TORNADO POTATO

Calvin Wong Tze Loon

黃子倫

As a kid, I'd lie on the floor and play *Risk* by myself, imagining a sci-fi future conflict with laser turrets and mechs duking it out over Australia. In 2004, I bought Rob Daviau's *Risk 2210* to live out my dreams of nuking the Moon with my friends.

It took another ten years before I would get into the hobby proper: posting about board games on social media.

Thus ensued:

- endless forum discussions on what games are suitable for grandmothers

- posting reviews of beloved games in my collection (*Android* by Kevin Wilson, *Chaos in the Old World* by Eric Lang)
- showing off my storage solutions and shelfies
- getting into fights about colonialism and cultural appropriation

As a result of all that (and especially because of that last bullet), I managed to make quite a few friends.

(Quick tip: Remember those names above, they become relevant later: Rob Daviau, Eric Lang, Kevin Wilson.)

One fateful August, one of my new friends from the internet messaged me.

> Hey Calvin, it's Raf
> Been doing some freelance writing for this board game website
> Heard you were looking for work
> Wanna do it too?

At the time I was doing a lot of part-time TV writing, which sounds glamorous but mostly consists of sitting at various surfaces with my laptop open, my body curled into increasingly prawn-like configurations as I tried to bring educational cartoon characters to life.

What I wrote back was:

> Hey, Raf, thanks for thinking of me! I'd love to try this out

But what I was actually saying was "Sign me up for five years of writing weekly board game news, Christmas Board Game Gift

Guides, Five Underrated Horror Games, and SEO-ranking game descriptions for every single Fantasy Flight Card Game Expansion Pack!"

I am still very proud of my work at BoardGamePrices.com, and my boss was a truly lovely man named Ben.

Perhaps too lovely, because when I pitched him the idea of flying my Malaysian butt out to Germany to cover the annual Spiel board game convention, he actually said yes.

Spiel, held in the west German (not West German) city of Essen, is the world's largest board game convention. In 2019 the attendance was 209,000 people, mostly Deutsche board game enthusiasts and their families. Prior to Ben very nicely saying yes, my impressions of the con came from high-angle floor photos on their website and hashtag-laden photos of exciting new titles. I would soon see for myself the kids' areas with bungee trampolines, colorful floor mats, and highly inventive kid's games involving giant 3D constructions and magnets. And tornado potatoes. More on that later.

I'd never been to Europe. My experience of travel was limited to the extremely fortunate six weeks I spent in Bahrain and Shanghai, right out of university, researching and writing for the World Expo in 2010 with the rest of the firm I was with at the time. I say this not as an indelicate method of dropping in my resume, but to highlight that at this point in my life I was fairly inexperienced at international travel.

And so, it was another fateful August when I booked tickets for my partner Dee and myself to go to Germany (via Amsterdam), arranged the accommodations, tried frantically to get my new mic to play nice with my phone, downloaded maps of the places we'd be staying, put translation software onto our phones, and fretted endlessly about whether "The name on your passport (Calvin Wong Tze Loon) must exactly match the name on the ticket (Wong Tze Loon Calvin)" rules would apply in the Europelands – or, worse, at the departing airport.

(In the writing business we call the previous two paragraphs foreshadowing.)

We somehow arrived in Amsterdam without incident and spent a couple of lovely days being very cold. Malaysia is 30o+ on average and Amsterdam was a lovely 15o. We were staying with a lady named Luisa and her very large and friendly cat – remember this was the halcyon days of 2016, when Airbnbs were a viable alternative to hotel living instead of a capitalist nightmare made flesh. We walked about downtown Amsterdam (no buildings more than four stories tall! So good!) ate poffertjes – a dessert I knew about from my work on the educational children's cartoon – and drank Heineken from the source. Part of my contract with Ben was to post coverage of the convention on Instagram and Twitter, so we'd brought a stuffed polar bear whom we decided would be our mascot for the trip: Colin the Board Game Bear. We took many amusing photos of him on various Dutch landmarks like the Albert Heijn shoe, and a packet of giant plastic french fries at Schiphol airport.

Then we got on a big bus to Germanland, marveled at passportless Schengen, got off the bus, took a train three stations north to Altenessen, got to the right street, and realized that I'd completely forgotten to write down the house number of the place we were staying.

"I remember what the front door looks like," I remember saying to a very stressed-out Dee as we wandered up and down a tiny street in the cold of deep autumn, but we were bailed out because the nice lady we were meant to be staying with had seen us from her window with our giant rolling bags and decided we were the ones. She and her husband lived with a very large dalmatian and rented out the apartment above their house. They spoke no English, so we had several very halting conversations where I would type "Can you drink the tap water?" into my phone and make it appear in German for the man, who would take my phone and squint very hard, then go "Ah, ja! Sie können das Wasser trinken! Gutes Wasser! Sehr gut!"

Or something like that. It was seven years ago.

We sat down for a bit because our feet hurt from all the walking and traveling. Dee had a little notebook where she was keeping track of all my scheduled meets and interviews. Penciled in for Day 0, right after "arrive," was a pre-Spiel dinner and games event at Unperfekthaus just a few train stops away.

So, we packed Colin and off we went. We availed ourselves of the lovely buffet and tried out some prototypes, nervously keeping an eye on the time we'd have to leave by in order to catch the last train.

"The train's closed," said the nice man at the bar when we asked him about 10:30 PM (2230 if you're German). "Where are you staying?"

"Altenessen," we told him.

"Ah, that's very near," he said. "Take the first bus outside."

We went outside. We asked the driver smoking a cigarette in front of the first bus.

"Second bus," he said, and pointed at the one behind him.

It was not the second bus. Watching our GPS dot move steadily further and further south, I told Dee we'd better get off the bus.

"According to this," I said, being very, very grateful that past Calvin had downloaded the map of the city to his phone, "it's thirty minutes' walk."

It was not thirty minutes. Traipsing for almost two hours

through the suburbs of Essen (a city of a half-million people) at nearly midnight in the autumn is surprisingly pleasant – when recalled several years after the fact. In the moment, Dee's foot was bleeding through her brand-new Nikes, I was developing some serious blisterage on both feet the day before we were due to cover a famously arch-destroying convention, and I was having to consult my phone at every junction just to make sure we were going the right way. Every darkened house, every gust of cold wind, every tick of my phone battery percentage was making the fear creep in. If it rained, I genuinely feared we might freeze to death.

"We're going to laugh about this later," I remember saying, when finally we saw the familiar train stations we'd ridden through on the way to the Airbnb and being cruelly reminded that ten minutes' train ride is much different on foot in the dark and cold. "Once our feet stop hurting."

So it was on very blistered feet that we took to Day 1 of the convention proper, armed with Colin, a DSLR camera, and internet access (which we had rushed to buy before going to Day 1).

I remember standing toward the back of the crowded train, feet hurting, looking around trying to distract myself from thinking about how many more stations it would be, and seeing a guy in a Board Game Ramblings t-shirt. Wait a minute. I know this person from the twitters!

"Johannes? Is that you?"

It totally was. He was on his way to Spiel too, and we finally got to meet in real life after being online friends for so long. This theme continued. All weekend we'd run into people we know from online and do the same little routine: "Oh my god, it's so nice to finally meet you!" "Oh my god you're so tall!" "Aaah, can we hug? We gotta hug!" "Hey, let's have lunch, I found this amazing stand out in the galleria that serves tornado potatoes… Yeah, I know right? It's a giant spiralized potato that's like two feet long and fried! You want one or two?"

Along with the giant box of fries from earlier, we were starting to get the message that the Europes were very into their potatoes.

And, honestly, part of me felt totally guilty about it. Remember at this point I was taking myself super-seriously as a board game journalist. I had just delivered one of the world's first reviews of *Scythe*, I was doing weekly features over at BoardGamePrices. com, and I had promised Ben professional coverage of this event. My appointment book had an entry every other hour. But somehow this all felt like a vacation rather than work. My heart was so full seeing all these people I was friends with from online, seeing designers whose games brought me into the hobby.

Looking back at it from years later is very weird. I vividly remember standing in the halls, consulting the little appointment book, when I saw a man with frizzy hair hustling out of a booth and chomping on an apple.

"Babe, I think that was Eric Lang."

"OMG, you should go say hi."

"Nah, he looks really busy. Anyway, I'm not even sure it was him."

(It was him.)

(Still wouldn't have said hi, though. He really did look really busy.)

One of the appointments in Dee's little book was Rob Daviau, who at the time was launching *Pandemic Legacy* and had agreed to an interview. In moments I was sitting there talking to one of the designers of another game that got me into board games.

I was a little nervous because I was new to the whole interview thing, but he was absolutely lovely. Rob gave a really long interview, made me feel like a real journalist, and even took a photo with Colin. (Lots of people took photos with Colin. Pro tip: bring a plush animal to conventions. People instantly remember who you are, and it makes for amazing photos.)

The thing is, I'm now designing a game. With Eric Lang. I'm friends with someone who made one of the first board games I ever played. (For the record, I asked him about the apple thing. He has no memory of it, but he confirms he was at Spiel that year, so it was probably him.)

The rest of the convention proceeded in a whirlwind. Before we knew it, we had somehow frantically uploaded podcasts, typed out previews, transcribed interviews, done four days of Spiel, and we were back home like it never really happened at all except for our memories of almost dying in the German autumn.

And then a funny thing happened with Ben.

"How would you feel about going again next year?"

Doing something once is a novelty but doing it again is habit forming. I started saying the names of random things in German as a joke. Taube! (Pigeon.) Groß Taube! (Big pigeon.) Ausgang! (Exit.) But it makes Dee laugh, so I keep doing it.

We ended up going to four Spiels, from 2016 to 2019. We met so many friends. We saw so many cool passion projects. One year was the anniversary of Martin Luther so we saw a bunch of games about Protestantism. There was a year where it felt like everyone was doing a Mars game. We ate so many tornado potatoes. Rachel and Heinze of *Semi Co-op* brought pins for Colin. I once chased T Caires down two halls to say hi. I shared chili con carne with Nikki Valens at the back of Hall 6. These people are still my friends, and the magic of Spiel helped it along.

One year after Spiel, we went to Berlin on the twenty-fifth anniversary of the fall of the Berlin Wall (Die Mauer). On the way to see the dinosaur museum, a car sped past us.

"Babe," I said as the police sirens faded away, "that was Angela Merkel."

"What was she doing?"

"From the way she was holding her phone, I think she was on Twitter."

And all this because of a random message I got from a friend because we posted on social media together.

The tens of thousands of words I wrote for BoardGamePrices. com have long since disappeared into the Interether. When I think back on the years we spent going to Spiel, before the pandemic, there's still an ache in my heart. I miss it dearly. Circumstances have yet to allow us to return without covid complications. But at least the memories won't disappear – memories of my friends, and the industry I now work in, and hopefully we will get to revisit soon.

Also, I did lie a bit right at the start when I said that Kevin Wilson's name would become relevant later, that wasn't totally true. We're now Twitter friends but we still haven't met.

But who knows, the crazy way things are going, it's only a matter of time before we're working together on something. Whatever it is, I hope it brings you joy the way games have done for me.

CALVIN WONG TZE LOON *is a board games writer who sometimes writes about board games. You may have read his words in* Twilight Imperium, Netrunner *or* PC Gamer, *and seen his face in* Crazy Rich Asians.

You can find Calvin on social media @ithayla

ROLL AND MOVE. (AGAIN.)

Donna Gregory

Easter Monday 1992 is a day for Bloody Scabs. My sister, Natalie, and I are exploring the sixty-story skyscraper we've just moved to in a hot, humid Hong Kong. Hong Kong is not just a new city, but a new continent, a new culture. We're excited to see that there's a swimming pool, then swiftly disappointed to note that it won't be open until next month. We try to play hide-and-go-seek in the deserted basement parking lot but get shooed away by the security guard. We walk up sixty flights of stairs to the very highest floor, where we're briefly awed by the windy rooftop views. There's not a lot to hold our attention, since we don't know what we're looking at, and it's not long before we find ourselves in the playground beside the building on the lookout for something to do in this strange new land. The sign on the playground says Nine And Under. We're ten and eleven. Not quite old enough to go out by ourselves in a big city, not quite young enough to play on the jungle gym. Our new school's semester doesn't start for another week, and we don't have any plans at all, except to get out of as many of the dull new-house chores as possible.

Natalie goes up to our new flat, where our parents are unloading the boxes and putting up our wobbly bunk bed. She lucks out with HK$20 in coins for the vending machine in the lobby, and grabs *Pass the Pigs* from our hand luggage. We're loudly struggling to work out the values of the novel, fluted-edged coins, and the potential merits of the exotic snacks on offer, when a girl passes by on rollerblades and tells us that the almond Pocky is the best. She nudges off the foam headphones of her yellow sports Walkman and offers to help. She's about our age, with an Australian accent. We invite her to share our vending machine bounty and play *Pass the Pigs* with us. *Pass the Pigs* is a success, and she invites us up to her apartment to play *Clue*. *Clue* soon segues into a riotous afternoon of our last school's favorite game – "Bloody Scabs."

Bloody Scabs was one of those apocryphal 90s folk games that children excitedly proclaimed had been banned at their cousin's neighbor's school, or swore on their life that a kid two towns over had died playing. I can't remember the exact rules, but it was basically Old Maid with consequences. Played with a regular deck of cards, when you drew a queen, you got to physically hit another player with the discard pile. There was a convoluted system for divining how many strikes you could deliver with the discard pile, how hard those strikes could be, who you'd get to hit, and whether they'd get to hit you back. My sister was a slicer, I was a scraper. The winner was the first to draw literal blood from another player. It sounds horrific – not to mention unhygienic – to my adult self, but as children we relished the small violence of it, and it bonded the three of us together as blood sisters. Thirty years later, Vending Machine Vickie is godmother to my sister's youngest daughter.

This is fairly typical of my life story. My dad worked for a credit card company, and his role was to install new computer hardware in their various offices and branches around the world. Each assignment would take anywhere from a couple of weeks to a few months, depending on the number of facilities within reach of his base. My mother had spent her childhood bouncing around England, South America, and the Caribbean, before she was orphaned at thirteen. My father and us children are her only family, and she didn't have a particular attachment to any geographical area, so I guess they decided it was best for us all to travel together to Dad's postings. Most of Mum's memories of her own mother were of playing *Scrabble* or card games together as they moved around from place to place, so she naturally taught us to play games, both to entertain ourselves and to break the ice with people we met along the way. Like my mother, I wasn't attached to any of the places we lived, so home for us was the games table. The scenery changed, but the games stayed the same.

And so, my sister and I frequently found ourselves enrolling in a new school. We're lucky enough to both be passably bright and relatively athletic, so the academic and sports sides of things were usually OK, but the social sphere was harder for me to repeatedly succeed in, especially as I got older. The craze of the new school might be anything from tarot to Tamagotchis, afterschool hangouts might include terrifying dance-offs at the basketball court or dipping salty fries in chocolate milkshakes at the geeky electronics mall, and, just like in the TV show

Quantum Leap, there was no way to prep for this in advance. Scrunchies or slouch socks might have been fashionable in Kuala Lumpur, but they might be mocked in Manila the very next month. In my favorite short-term school in Kathmandu, there was a lunchtime *Scrabble* club, and at most schools there would be a chess club, but I was never good enough at chess to endure the stigma of being the only girl in the room.

Best of all was when we joined at the tail end of a school term, during that week where each teacher either wheeled in the big TV and put on a movie or let the class play beaten-up board games with questionable educational value instead of learning about oxbow lakes or the Roman Empire. This gave me a valuable chance to make a local friend to hang out with over the upcoming school break, someone to have fun and hopefully play more games with, and also to help me to navigate my new environment.

The internet didn't become universal until fairly late in my high school career, and even then it was mostly used for messaging, flame wars and dancing baby memes. There was no Google Maps, no Tripadvisor, no top-ten listicles to find out what there was to do in a new place. In the bigger cities, the library might have some guidebooks or magazines, but they were always written by stuffy adults with very different interests to children. Better than a guidebook was a human guide – a cheat code kid who, in addition to being willing to play *Loot* or *Connect 4* or even *Bloody Scabs*, might invite me to dip into their own games closet. Critically, they probably also knew valuable intangibles like which bus to take to get to the waterpark, which mall the scary kids hung out in, which park the wheezy nerds were safe in, and which convenience store had the best variety of soda.

If I didn't luck out with a board game school day, I needed to actively seek out a new local buddy. In each new school, there would be hundreds of students in already-established cliques and social hierarchies. How was I to identify a potential friend, someone to help me navigate the social scene and tell me what to wear to that all-school mixer on Friday – the dungarees-and-Docs combo, or the bike shorts and Hypercolor t-shirt? When I was really little, I could simply sidle over to pretty much any other same-size-ish kid and ask if they wanted to play, or even if they straight up wanted to be my friend. As a teen, I needed a more sophisticated strategy, so I deployed board games as a friend-finding system. I took to carrying a small, super-easy game in my backpack, something like a *Top Trumps* deck or a travel version of *Guess Who?*, and if I could find a kid or two who looked non-threatening and a little bored in a break period, I would offer the game up as a sneaky way to get to know people, and get the inside track on the new scene I found myself in.

That first game bought me precious time to work out if any of my opponents were likely to like me, and gave me a chance to see if I might like them, too. Essentially, it was an interview, an audition, but without the formal questions, and with a much higher chance of some incidental fun. Would one of my opponents be the annoying sort who reads the rule booklet silently from cover to cover, and then debates the merits of each starting setup for so long that it's time to go home for tea before you've even rolled the first dice? Are they a to-be-avoided drip, hoping that someone else will take charge? Are they really good at math, or drawing, or English (and therefore might it be useful to try to get paired with them in class)? Are they likely to pitch a fit if they can't be the blue tokens, or if I don't want to play their weird made-up rules?

In the small group of a tabletop game, there's no big crowd to impress or compete with for attention. I knew I would have at least a half hour to settle in, so the pressure of the first impression was lessened a little. I also never had to repeat the experience, if the game didn't go well and I didn't see the potential for a friendship.

Helpfully, there is also a literal code for the interaction, with written rules from start to finish that are the same for everyone, even if they're brand new to the table. It's a level playing field, and it buys me an hour or two of potential pals' time. As a slightly anxious teen girl, the idea of being the focus of someone's attention is utterly abhorrent, but when we're playing a game, I'm not the sole focus, I'm in the much safer peripheral gaze. This gave me time to observe, to build some shared experiences, and to find the chink in the friendship circle through which I might enter and be accepted.

If I was lucky, I'd find someone with the imagination and verve I was looking for to make our time as friends memorable. I vividly remember falling in instant friend-love with April, in Australia, whose family set of *Clue* had been customized in the cutest way, with homemade cards featuring their six dogs, so you wound up accusing Mr Merlin, the fifteen year-old hairy wolfhound, of murdering most awfully Miss Mittens-the-Kitten with the Stolen Sock in the Boot Room. As they'd renamed the board's rooms after spaces in their own home, to make a declaration you had to drag the whole crew to the actual room in which you believed the deed had been done, something that incensed her much-cooler older brothers when a gaggle of giggling nine year-old girls burst into their private spaces.

It's a good job I have board games as a strategy for making friends, because when you often start over, you're often lonely, at least for a spell. Humans aren't good at saying straight out that we find ourselves friendless and need to spend time with people. There has to be a reason, an excuse. "I'm lonely, please will you hang out with me?" is an uncomfortable thing to say out loud, and it's probably not an easy thing to hear either. We might all feel that way sometimes, but we often look for ways to not admit it because that admission is of a very visceral vulnerability. Even if you leave out the part about being lonely, everyone still hears it. Loneliness is, I think, often unconsciously thought of as contagious, so it's risky to say that you want to spend time with someone, even if both of you would like it to happen. "Fancy coming over for a game of *Wingspan*?" is a less direct way of saying "I'd like to be friends, please!" that doesn't reek of desperation. It can be about the game, and the companionship gained can be a happy bonus.

I honed my board-game-as-friend-filter scheme through the transience of university halls and early adulthood. In the summer I turned nineteen, I spent the long university break in Greece. I got a job in a café on a beach in Naxos after beating the owner at backgammon while waiting to check in to my hostel, and I continued to play him and his friends at tiny, smoky tables for four months, while occasionally deigning to make coffee or pour Metaxa for customers. The following Christmas, I got a temporary job as a location producer for a travel TV show in Morocco, and spent hours and hours playing *Carcassonne* with the crew in a hot riad courtyard while making endless calls on a huge satellite phone and filing rushes through unstable internet connections. I abandoned my second-year exams (I still passed, though to this day I am not entirely sure how) to crew yachts in Croatia, where I learned that *Ticket to Ride* is not the game to play in rough seas.

I wrote my dissertation while cycling from England to Italy, because I found it easier to think while riding my bike than in a library full of stressed-out students. I would review my notes and research while I had coffee or lunch, compose paragraphs in my head on the move, then scribble them down in a ditch by the side of the road during water breaks. Due to the need to carry the copious sheaves of sources and notes I'd photocopied before setting off, I didn't have room in my panniers for more than a set of dominoes. I had a minor mishap in the Swiss Alps, when my bike and everything I owned fell down a scree slope. When I reached the hostel in Verona where I finally emailed off the finished dissertation, I went to play a celebratory game of dominoes over pasta in the sticky kitchen with some people from my dorm, but I realized I had lost a lot of the tiles (and, inconveniently, my passport). We played anyway, and it didn't matter that the set was incomplete, possibly because my new friends and I had bought quite a lot of cheap fizzy wine to celebrate the end of the dissertation.

Through my early adult life, I moved more than forty times. I don't have strong ties anywhere, so it was easy to move when rent got too expensive, a relationship broke down, a job contract expired, a better offer appeared, or I just got a little restless.

As I established myself in the world of work, I was pleased to find that there are plenty of folk who don't think of tabletop games as child's play. I could casually drop into kitchen conversation at a new job that I like swimming, movies, and playing *Ticket to Ride*. If my coffee-making companion wasn't into board games, they'd focus on either the swimming or the movies, but if they were a gamer, it would often be enough for them to propose a lunchtime round of *King of Tokyo* or even a pub evening of *Tzolkin*, a tactic that has led to several of my more permanent and valued friendships. This did backfire once, when I merrily agreed to play *CATAN* with a new line manager and a couple of others in a trendy brewery after work one day. It soon became clear that my boss was incredibly indecisive, took ages for each of his turns, and nearly cried when the Robber stole his resources. I had been excited to join his team, but I found it harder to collaborate with him on day-to-day editorial tasks after I realized that his dithering affected us at work, too.

Over the pandemic, something shifted for me, as I'm sure it did for a lot of people. Some subtle alchemy of turning forty, of being legally required to stay in one place for a while, of the pre-vaccine fear of getting sick, of Zoom *Pictionary* sessions, of getting a puppy who never had a chance to learn how to be alone, and of the great freedoms and possibilities offered up by working remotely resulted in the decision to make one last big move (I know, the absolute Covid cliché of it all). And so, last summer, I picked up my needy little Ivy-dog, loaded my possessions into a van and moved five hundred miles to the next country over, to the seventy-first, and hopefully final, home of my life.

I'm delighted to be back near my sister and her family again, and we immediately started up Friday Night Game Night, though she can't be my only entertainment. My far-flung friends make plans to visit, but I'm in need of some regular in-person pals. What else is there to do but call round to my new neighbors and message the new softball team to issue invites to a *CATAN* night? I probably won't be needing the wrinkled deck of bloodstained playing cards this time round.

DONNA GREGORY *is an editor specializing in non-fiction, and has worked for publishers including Routledge, Bonnier, and Quarto on titles including* Brick City, The Outdoor Kama Sutra *and* The Story of Life. *After living in more than seventy different places over the first forty years of her life, she now lives on the west coast of Scotland.*

THE MAGIC CIRCLE

Matt Coward-Gibbs

When was the last time that you played a game with other people? I am going to assume it was somewhat recently, given that you're reading a book about what board games mean to people. I'm also going to hazard a guess that you were sat around a table, with some friends or family, and that while you were playing you were focused on the game and the interactions you were having with the other people you were playing with. For that brief period, most other things happening around you might have slipped away and become less important than what you were doing.

Within games studies, this phenomenon is known as "the magic circle." It has been discussed in research about games since Johan Huizinga's *Homo Ludens* was first published in 1938. In defining what the magic circle is, he wrote that: "...all play moves and has its beginnings within a playground marked off beforehand either materially or ideally, deliberately or as a matter of course."

From what Huizinga tells us, we might start to think of the magic circle as being something that people agree to enter: going through a door into a room and leaving everything else from the "real world" behind. For someone to be part of a magic circle – or to take part in a game – they must be aware that they are playing. Importantly, the way that this is done can look different for different types of play. These playgrounds that Huizinga speaks about can be very clear. For example, the five people around a Pandemic board are entering a magic circle, in which there has been a deliberate agreement to play the game. In roleplaying games, people are agreeing to suspend reality and enter play.

At its simplest, the magic circle is an imaginary space that people enter when they engage in play. When in this space, if a group of people come together, and engage in a game, where they share the same social space and identity. However, what this has led to at this point is a near-century of arguments about what exactly *the magic circle* is. At its broadest, we might consider the magic circle as a way of developing a community: a way of bringing a group of like-minded people together. At its simplest, that is what we are as board gamers: we are a community. And as a community, we use the games we play (and the magic circles we create) to build relationships with other people.

In some cases, such as within roleplaying games, systems have been developed to make sure that the magic circle is working for everybody. Although such practices are more commonly found within roleplaying games, we also see them being deployed within board game play, especially within large-scale public events such as national conventions.

Recently, we have seen a rise in activities aimed to develop accessible and equitable magic circles for players. These activities and practices are sometimes more widely described as being safety measures. However, in essence, what they do is create a shared space in which power (who is in control of the magic circle) is distributed equally. One of the most recognized ways in which this is practiced is through the use of an X Card. This is a physical card placed on the table that can be touched by anyone playing when they feel uncomfortable. Although the X Card is a very visible sign that someone is not enjoying their experience, it is still reliant on the magic circle (that shared community ethos) and that others playing will be willing to change what is taking place, to support the player who is feeling uncomfortable.

Another safety measure we might want to think about is "Lines and Veils," a system developed by Ron Edwards as part of a supplement for his roleplaying game, *Sorcerer*. More formalized than the X Card, this measure asks players to think about what the lines that cannot be crossed are, and what can be alluded to (veils). Let's use an example: say a player has arachnophobia, the inclusion of spiders within the game would most likely be a line (something which cannot be crossed). However, if the same player instead just didn't like spiders, it could be veiled: spiders exist in the world that they are playing in, but they are not directly interacted with during the game. Lines and Veils creates a space of ongoing negotiation of lines and veils among all players during a game, to create a space which is welcoming to all who want to play.

Over time, what became clear was that when you enter a magic circle, you don't leave everything at the door; in fact, you take all your life experiences and relationships into the game with you. The same happens when you leave, you take away all the connections you've made and the experiences that you have had. Where the real magic happens is that when you enter and exit the magic circle, you have engaged in a space where playing a game can impact the "real world." We've seen this time and time again in the way board games have been used to help nurses and other medical professionals develop and hone their problem-solving skills. Or how in many conversations I've had over the years, neurodiverse people have spoken to me about how much they feel their communication skills have grown through playing games. Having a fixed ruleset to play within has meant they feel more comfortable being social and interacting with people.

If we think about the magic circle as entering a doorway, it allows us to think about the way in which the games we play, and what we learn and experience, can have a positive impact in our everyday lives. These magic circles become spaces of transformation in multiple ways. For example, Salen and Zimmerman write in their game design textbook *Rules of Play*, that once the "game begins, everything changes. Suddenly the materials represent something quite specific. The plastic token is you. These rules tell you how to roll the dice and move. Suddenly, it matters very much which plastic token reaches the end first."

The fact that we can enter new worlds by gathering around a board might be considered somewhat magical in itself. That, in a single instance, we might be able to become those tasked with saving the world (in Pandemic), commanders of empires (in the likes of *Scythe* or *Root*), or even just day-to-day people who are tasked with organizing their bookcases (in *My Shelfie*).

Let me give you an example. Let me tell you about my friend Alys. After finishing her degree, Alys moved to China to teach English as a second language. Board gaming had been one of the main ways that she socialized while at university in the UK. Having settled into her new apartment in mainland China, Alys was glad to find out that her new housemates were also interested in board games. During winter break, Alys and her housemates settled down in their apartment to begin a campaign of *Pandemic Legacy: Season 1*.

For those of you unfamiliar with the game, it involves two to four players working cooperatively as a team of specialists attempting to eradicate several diseases before they infect the globe. Players must work together, and are required to move around the globe, build research centers, treat diseases, block transmission, and hopefully eradicate diseases by finding a cure. Legacy games like *Pandemic Legacy: Season 1* are primarily narrative driven and present an overarching story that is developed across multiple sessions of play (between twelve and twenty-four games in the case of *Pandemic Legacy*). Yet, what was interesting about the way Alys and her housemates played was how they went about tailoring the experience for themselves. Alys told me that they "bought doctors' masks and little petri dishes to put the cubes in and little biohazard bags and stuff. They added to the occasion, but it didn't affect the gameplay."

By using props, they made *a* game into *their* game. Like Alys said, "it's more personal, you've personally changed the board, you've named the characters, you've named the diseases ... that's always fun, I'm pretty sure one of our diseases was called 'capitalism.'"

By making changes to the board in *Pandemic Legacy* (drawing connections between locations, applying stickers) and removing components from the game (physically destroying cards) each campaign becomes unique for the players. Physically changing the board and destroying things, however, sits quite uneasy with a lot of gamers – Alys included – because of the level of care that is usually afforded to their games. Yet, the alteration of the board during this campaign meant that something interesting took place. When they'd finished the game, Alys and her friends framed the board. "That was really nice. We stuck loads of cards onto it and put it all up in a big Perspex frame. I want to play a legacy game again with my friends here, I suspect I'll do the same at the end..."

Once you complete the campaign of a *Pandemic Legacy* game, the physical components are rendered near-useless. Converting the game into a piece of wall art makes a statement of the shared experiences across play. Not only has Alys's game been memorialized, but it offers a tangible representation of the shared experiences and accomplishments garnered during its play. Importantly, for Alys, it demonstrates a way in which her housemates became her friends.

So, what do board games mean to me? Well, at their most fundamental they are an opportunity to be social. To engage in play in a space with an agreed set of rules, where the social expectations are clear to the players. More than that, games offer a wealth of opportunities for their players. There are chances to build and develop social and communal bonds. There are opportunities to learn about the world we live in. Games offer the opportunity to take on different roles and to try out new things within spaces that are safe. The magic circle is this space for transformation, a space that, simply put, allows for the good stuff! For me, this is the purpose of the magic circle. It provides the opportunity to bring people together on a shared and level playing field.

MATT COWARD-GIBBS *is a lecturer in Sociology and Criminology at York St John University. He is a member of the investigate.games research group. Matt's research considers the importance of play, fun and games in the social world. He is the editor of* Death, Culture and Leisure: Playing Dead *(Emerald, 2020).*

You can find more about Matt's work at investigate.games

GATEWAYS TO GAMING

Jervis Johnson

Board games mean so much to me that it is hard to know where to start! When I think about how I became a gamer, what comes into my mind quite vividly are the shops where I bought my first board games. When I started gaming back in the late 1960s, there was no internet and precious few gaming magazines, so my gateway to the board gaming hobby was what I found in the local store.

The first shop I can remember buying games from was a toy shop about fifteen minutes' walk from my home with the enticing name of Toys, Toys, Toys. It was a wonderful place that was crammed with toys of all varieties and for all age ranges. I used to go there quite regularly to spend my pocket money, more so after I was old enough to go out on my own (which, this being the late 1960s, was once I was about eight or nine years old). I can't remember why I was drawn toward the board games, which were hidden away in the back of the shop alongside its jigsaws, but I was. My first purchase was a game called *Wild Life*. The somewhat politically incorrect object of the game was to travel round a map of the world collecting different sorts of animal for your zoo. Now, it has to be said that *Wild Life* was not a groundbreaking piece of games design, even back then, but it was perfectly serviceable. It clearly made a big impact on me because I can remember the box, board and (especially) the playing cards from the game to this day. My sister and I played *Wild Life* a lot, and soon enough I was back in Toys, Toys, Toys looking for another game. Although I didn't know it at the time, I had taken the first steps on what would become a lifelong hobby.

Image: Eàmon Bloomfield

The second game I remember getting from Toys, Toys, Toys was called *Exploration*. The objective of *Exploration* was to equip and then carry out one of four different expeditions to a so-far-undiscovered location. Like *Wild Life*, *Exploration* was a simple game, but to my ten year-old self it was quite mind-blowing. I remember thinking that it was exciting and that the theme of the game was well executed, and I loved the special die that came with the game, which was used to regulate movement. The fact that there were four expeditions you could go on, each of which was slightly different, gave it a lot of replay value. With *Exploration* I was hooked, and although I didn't realize it then, I was going to keep on playing board games for the rest of my life.

Over the years I've thought often about what it was that drew me to the hobby, and I've come to the conclusion that it was the sense of structure that games offer. I was an anxious child, who found the world a chaotic and confusing place that was difficult to cope with. It seemed to me that there was no way of understanding the things that happened in my life, and because of that I longed for structure and some form of control. Games offered that to me – they had rules, and the rules gave me a way of understanding and predicting what would or could happen as they were being played. When I played a game, I could understand how at least one little bit of my world worked, and with this understanding came the chance, to some extent at least, to be in control of things. It was a real comfort to me then, and it still is now.

The third game I remember buying from Toys, Toys, Toys was an altogether different beast called *4000 AD*. This game was released in 1972, which means I would have been twelve or thirteen years old when I got it. By this time, I was already playing miniature wargames using Airfix toy soldiers, so I had moved on a bit from family games like *Wild Life* and *Exploration*. Nonetheless, I remember *4000 AD.* as being a complex game. I had been drawn to the game by its theme: it was a strategic wargame where the players were trying to conquer the galaxy. I liked wargaming and I liked science fiction, so the game was a natural fit for me. The game itself was highly innovative for its time. It used a form of hidden movement, and the board had a "3D" element to it, in that some spaces were considered to be one space above or below the playing surface. On the downside, the playing pieces were fiddly to use, and the combat system was simplistic even to my teenage mind (the side with fewer pieces in a battle was wiped out, with no losses to the other side). Nonetheless I enjoyed the game, even if I don't have as soft a spot for it as I do for *Wild Life* and *Exploration*.

In 1974, my family moved across London from Swiss Cottage to Kilburn. This introduced me to the second shop that provided me with a gateway into the gaming hobby. Bivouac Books was located on Kilburn High Road, about a twenty minute walk from my house. Up until this point, most of my games had been played against my sister and my friend, Ciaron, both of whom enjoyed games but weren't obsessed with them like I was. I needed to find other people who liked playing games in the same way that I did, and Bivouac Books helped to do so. I had come across Bivouac Books by chance one day and was drawn to the selection of SPI games that were on sale, which looked a combination of the Second World War tabletop wargame rules I was using and *4000 AD*. Soon I was the owner of a game called *Kampfpanzer* and another called *Kursk*. Neither game appealed to my sister or Ciaron, so I was incredibly lucky to make friends with a fellow wargamer at my school. He had a copy of an SPI game called *Panzer Armee Afrika*, so we played that and my two games, forging a friendship that continues to this day. There weren't any other gamers at my school, but with the help of the staff at Bivouac Books and through the small ads that appeared in magazines like *Military Modelling*, I was able to contact more gamers. This friendship group was incredibly important to me, because as well as being an anxious child, I was a shy and rather withdrawn one too, and playing games gave me a chance to socialize and make friends.

Toy, Toys, Toys and Bivouac Books each had a profound effect on my life, but it was another shop, that I discovered a little later, that had the greatest impact. It was called Games Centre, and it was the first "proper" games shop I visited. I found out about Games Centre through the pages of *Games & Puzzles* magazine, which I had finally come across on the racks of a local newsagent. I didn't know it at the time, but *Games & Puzzles* was published by Graeme Levin, who just happened to be the owner of Games Centre, and therefore the magazine had several large adverts for the store. Both Toys, Toys, Toys and Bivouac Books had been within easy walking distance of my house, but Games Centre was located quite a long way away in Central London. Nothing daunted, I set off on my trusty pedal bike and made the ten mile round trip to the store, somehow managing not to get run over as I cycled the busy London streets. What I discovered at the end of this journey was a cornucopia of games: board games, wargames, roleplaying games, classic games, games imported from all round the world, books about games, gaming accessories, and on and on and on. I was in heaven. From then on, I visited Games Centre as often as I could, either to browse or to play games at the Saturday games club held at a café nearby.

Games Centre acted as a hub for the gaming community, and I made new friends and found out about all kinds of different games to play, but it also ended up providing me with a career when I came across a small ad for a job at Games Centre. I applied for the position, and much to my surprise I was successful! I've come to realize that as you go through life, there are things that happen which seem quite small at the time but will help to determine your future. That job at Games Centre was one of those things for me. I can truly say that I wouldn't be sitting here writing this chapter if I hadn't spotted that small ad and applied for the job. I started out at Games Centre working in the office compiling the information received in a recent *Games & Puzzles* survey, before moving on to work in the shop as a sales assistant. Just a few years later, a friend from Games Centre offered me a job at Games Workshop, where I worked until my retirement a couple of years ago. My wife often says that I am obsessed with games and disappear into my own little world when I am playing them or creating them. I think this is true, especially when I am trying to find the solution to an especially knotty game design problem. Just as playing games when I was younger offered me a chance to escape a world that seemed chaotic and dangerous, designing games for Games Workshop allowed me to do so during my working day – and much of my free time as well! I would never have got the chance to do that were it not for the lessons I learned while I was at Games Centre.

But Games Workshop lay in my future. Throughout my time at Games Centre I was, of course, playing games, lots and lots of games, but there are three games that stand out from that time because of the lessons I learned from them about games design. The first of these games was called *Black Box*. It was a clever asymmetric game for two players, where one player hid a set of four atoms somewhere in an 8 x 8 grid of squares, and their opponent had to discover their location by firing imaginary "rays" into the grid. *Black Box* was very popular in its day (I remember selling dozens of copies) but has faded from sight since then. This is a shame, because it really is a very clever piece of game design that takes what is really a pure abstract game and makes it much more accessible by giving the abstract mechanics a great theme. I was lucky enough to meet the game's designer, Eric Solomon, and get to playtest some of his other games, and I learned a lot in the process, not the least of which is that games design is great fun!

The second game that stands out for me from my time at Games Centre is *Cosmic Encounter*. In the game, up to six players vie to conquer the galaxy by being the first to capture five of their opponents' planets. I first got to play *Cosmic Encounter* at one of the games review sessions that were held in Games Centre's offices after work on Thursday nights. These sessions were used to test out new games for the reviews that appeared in *Games & Puzzles* magazine, and whenever I have played *Cosmic Encounter* since then I find my mind wandering back to them.[1] As a younger member of the team I didn't get to write any of the reviews, but I did get to play lots and lots of different games, and to help playtest games with the likes of Eric. The chats about the games after we had played them required me to analyze what it was that I liked about a game, and then express that view to the other players. It was a seminal experience and set me in good stead for when I was designing and playtesting games for Games Workshop later in my career. As the famous phrase goes, "Artists steal, amateurs merely

---

1 Interestingly *Cosmic Encounter* split the reviewers into lovers (like me) and haters, so when it was reviewed it got a pretty mediocre review and score. Fortunately, the lovers were proved right in the long term, and *Cosmic Encounter* has remained available pretty much continuously since it first came out back in 1977.

copy." The trick is to steal ideas to create something new rather than to just imitate what came before.

A good example of this is a game mechanic I stole – sorry, I mean *learned* – from a game called *Speed Circuit*. As its name implies, *Speed Circuit* is a car racing game. Each player is the driver of a Formula 1 racing car, which they "drive" around a racing track – there were different game boards for each of the F1 racing tracks – and the player whose car comes in first is the winner. *Speed Circuit* is a quick-playing and rather accessible game, and I played it a lot with my colleagues at Games Centre and my friends outside work. One of the things I liked best about the game was that you could either move safely round the track, or risk going a bit faster. The problem with going fast was that you had to roll a die to avoid spinning out. Of course, if you didn't take any risks, you would probably lose to players that did, so the trick was to drive in a way that minimized the need to roll the dice, and to only make a roll if you absolutely had to. It's a clever feature because it means that you can't blame losing the game on bad luck – after all, you didn't have to roll the dice if you didn't want to! This principle lodged itself in my brain and I ended up using it when I designed *Blood Bowl*, which, for example, has a rule that allows players to move an extra square or two, but at the risk they may roll a 1 and fall down.

So, when someone asks me "What do board games meant to you?", my answer is that they mean much more to me than just a way to pass the time, or because they are a mental challenge, or an engrossing hobby. They are all those things to me, but they also helped me cope with what seemed to be a chaotic and threatening world; they gave me a way to make friends and avoid my feelings of loneliness, and they provided me with a fulfilling and satisfying career. I would have found none of these things were it not for the owners and staff of Toys, Toys, Toys, and Bivouac Books, and Games Centre: I owe them all an immeasurable debt. I know I am not alone in this, either amongst my peers back then in the 1970s, or the myriad of gamers that have joined the hobby since then. Even in this internet age, local shops remain a vital gateway for people to discover and participate in the board gaming hobby. In my hometown of Nottingham, stores like Waterstones and John Lewis stock a good selection of board games, newsagents like WH Smith sell magazines about the gaming hobby, and there are two games cafés where people can buy games and hire gaming tables to play them on. Knowing that these shops are around makes me happy, both because I get a chance to browse the games that are on sale (and what gamer doesn't love doing that?), but also because they I know they are introducing a new generation of gamers to board games, just as Toys, Toys, Toys, and Bivouac Books, and Games Centre did for me.

So, the next time you visit your friendly local games shop, take a minute or two to consider just how lucky you are to have it, and maybe take a moment to thank the people that run it. They deserve our gratitude.

JERVIS JOHNSON *was a member of Games Workshop's Design Studio for more than thirty years until his retirement in 2021 and is best known as the designer of* Blood Bowl, *as well as* Epic *and* Warhammer Age of Sigmar. *He has been a keen games player for as long as he can remember.*

WHERE SHALL WE PLAY?

Leslie Scott

I was born and raised in Africa. Because of that, there are certain books and certain board games that, while in no way reflecting my life in Africa, still trigger some of the strongest memories I have of my family and my African childhood.

Cluedo and My Cousins

Despite its mustard-yellow colonels, plum-purple professors, its 1930s English country house setting and the Agatha Christie-like murder-mystery of the game itself, for me, playing *Cluedo* (*Clue*, to US readers) always evokes the time I was introduced to the game in a remote bush house on the banks of the Naro Moru river, a crystal-clear, cold trout stream that tumbles down the slopes of Mount Kenya.

Rather grandly dubbed "the Fishing Lodge," this country retreat on the equator was a bumpy three-hour drive from our home in Nairobi. It was not much more than a rickety wooden hut with a rusty corrugated iron roof and few amenities. There was no running water indoors and the long drop was several steps from the back door; several steps too many to risk in the dark for me and my younger sister, especially when we knew that it was entirely possible that we could encounter a prowling, hungry leopard or step on a sleepy, ill-tempered puff adder.

A family of warthogs lived under the house, and though usually quiet enough, there would be the occasional intense and noisy scuffle, which would send plumes of red dust up through the gaps in the floorboards of the lodge's one and only reception room, to settle thickly on the dining table, overstuffed armchairs and the shelf of old paperback novels left by previous weekender fisherfolk.

I still play *Cluedo* with pleasure, but I must confess that it is very hard for me to disentangle this lasting appreciation for the game from the very fond recollections of playing it that weekend with my family, my two considerably older cousins in particular.

Although their home was only a short distance from us in Nairobi, we seldom spent time with these half-Dutch cousins as they both boarded at schools "overseas" – that is, in England. As a consequence, they seemed so otherworldly and exotic, and I idolized them. The very fact that they deigned to be there that long weekend made this a special enough occasion: that they spent the evenings first teaching, then playing a board game with me and my siblings was remarkable; that this game was *Cluedo* made it unforgettable. The brilliance and joy of this game is that having got the hang of it, it really can be played as equals by all ages. By the end of the weekend, I had won at least one game fair and square, and was hooked.

It has been said that to play a game means entering into a magic circle, a space in which the normal rules and reality of the world are suspended and replaced by the reality of a game world. I believe something genuinely magical happened while we played *Cluedo* that weekend. It cast a spell so powerful that, almost sixty years on, I can still hear the hiss and smell – the pungent aroma – of the paraffin lantern that encircled the five of us in a warm glow, leaving everything around us in shadow.

Chinese Checkers and My Grandmother

My mother's mother was a ubiquitous and well-loved, if slightly formidable, figure throughout my childhood and into my early twenties. It didn't seem to matter where we were living (and we lived in many different places in many different African countries), there was always a Granny's room, flat or cottage in our home. I know now that she couldn't possibly have resided with us throughout the year as she spent a good deal of time with my uncle's family on their farm in South Africa, and my aunt's family (of the cousins above) wherever they were living at the time (they moved about East Africa as much as we did). But perhaps it feels as though she was always with us because, wherever we were, "Granny's room" was always an out-of-bounds and therefore tantalizing place that you could only enter when lucky enough to be invited to visit her to play a game of Chinese checkers.

I had always believed that this game had been given to my grandmother by my grandfather (who had died long before I was born), who had lived in China as a young man. It was only researching for this piece that I discovered that the Pressman Company of America first published what they referred to as Chinese Checkers in 1928, and that it was based on an 1892 German game called Sternhalma (because of its star-shaped board). This was itself a simplified version of the American game of halma, which was played on a square board and patented in 1888 by an American thoracic surgeon called George Monks. According to some accounts, his inspiration for halma (which means "jump") may have been an English game called hoppity, although there is no evidence that hoppity ever existed at all. It is clear, however, that Chinese checkers has nothing whatsoever to do with the game of checkers or China! I can't recall playing any other game with my grandmother, although she was a redoubtable bridge player all her long life. I don't remember playing Chinese checkers with anyone else, or anywhere else other than in her room, or on anything else other than her hexagram-shaped wooden board with its very beautiful, polished stone marbles; ten each of six different colors. I can still hear the clack-clack-clack sound of stone on wood as we took turns to hop a marble across the board to the opposite side.

It is very likely that at some time or another, I would have played Chinese checkers with my grandmother in almost every one of the "Granny's rooms" of the dozen or more homes my family lived in when I was a child. As these rooms were always identically furnished with Granny's belongings, in my mind they have merged into just the one room. Even so, there is one in Uganda that I remember in sharper detail than all the others, possibly because it was a detached, red-brick, metal-roofed cottage that was reached via a long cement path full of cracks. I was only five years old, so remember only odd snippets of our life in Kampala (we moved to Nairobi, Kenya, before I was six). Yet, I clearly recall dashing down this path in the rain to visit Granny to play Chinese checkers, taking great care to avoid stepping on cracks for fear of waking a bear in its lair. It is so strange that, given the possibility of encountering any number of very real and dangerous creatures, we were warned against *bears* – there are no bears in Africa.

In my mind's eye, I can distinctly recall the incredibly loud noise of the rain on the hot tin roof, and clearly see my grandmother and me sitting across from each other on two identical chairs, with the Chinese checkers board laying between us on a marquetry table. This lovely little table, which I'm guessing is English, now belongs to one of my brothers. (I re-upholstered the chairs and have them in my bedroom today.)

Up against one whitewashed wall, I can picture the brass-studded, wooden Zanzibar chest (which my sister owns now) and hanging above it, a large and very striking oil painting of an old woman, which I inherited from my mother a few years ago. Of course, I didn't know this at the time, nor indeed until many, many years later, but apparently my grandmother "won" this rather fine painting in 1942 when she bought a raffle ticket for a few shillings at a fundraiser in Dar es Salaam. Funds were being raised to help support the tens of thousands of Polish refugees, many of whom were women and children, who had fled war-torn Europe for the relative safety of East Africa.

To one side of this painting was a much smaller watercolor, painted by my great-great uncle (my grandfather's uncle) who had helped my grandparents purchase land in 1920 in the Southern Highlands of Tanganyika, now Tanzania. It was here that, while my grandfather and his uncle were away (unsuccessfully) panning for gold in the Lupa river, my grandmother planted and nurtured the first seedlings of the tea farm on which my mother was born. The painting, which my other brother now owns, is of the view of Lake Nyasa (also known as Lake Malawi) from the veranda of the house they built. I don't know if this house is still there, but I believe this tea plantation – the first in that region – thrives to this day.

I can think of many other artifacts of my grandmother that would have been present in that room in Uganda, and every one of her rooms thereafter; each one with its own story that formed a part of my grandmother's own story, and down the line via my mother, of my own story, too.

In *almost* all instances I could tell you where and with whom each one of these items now resides; as for example the original copy of passport No 6, a single-page document, issued to my grandfather on February 21, 1913, by "His Britannic Majesty's Vice Consul at Peking" to "request and require in the name of His Majesty that all those to whom it concern allow Alexander Charles Masters aged 24 to pass freely and without let or hindrance as he travels to and from England via Siberia." This historically significant document (passport No 6, no less!) is framed and hanging in my home where I can and do see it every day, which goes some way to explain why I had always thought Chinese checkers were, well, Chinese.

However, in the case of that Chinese checkers game, I haven't a clue where her game board and stone marbles are now. So, it is lucky that I only need to think of this game for the memories of my grandmother to come flooding in.

Battleships and My Father

Although my father played many games with me and my siblings, the one that instantly comes to mind when I think of him is a pencil and paper game he called Battle of Britain, which is identical to Battleships. Dad must have taught me this game of hide-and-seek from the moment I could grasp the concept of using a grid, because I have a very clear memory of playing it with him in a beach house in Kenya soon after I turned seven.

My beloved father left England for East Africa years before I was born, and only came "home" to England when I was in my early twenties, and just a few months before he died. Therefore, it isn't surprising that, even now, I never really think of Dad as having been British or *from* England.

I must have always known that he had been a fighter pilot in the Royal Air Force in England during World War II, as this would surely have come up when he taught me this Battle of Britain game. After all, it involved placing warplanes of different sizes (that is, taking up different number of squares) in the grid, the names of which still resonate with me now – Hurricane, Mustang, Mosquito, Whirlwind, Lancaster, Wellington, and of course, Spitfire, the famous single-seater plane that he flew.

As a child, I couldn't possibly have understood what it meant to have fought a war at all, let alone in the air and, although I've seen photos of him in uniform from that time, I still find it hard enough to imagine my father was ever aged eighteen, let alone the reckless daredevil that he must have been; all Spitfire pilots were, apparently. Less difficult to envisage is him as the skillful, quick-witted, fearless flyer with excellent eyesight that were necessary traits of the fighter pilot, too, in particular for any that survived the war. A great many did not.

Luckily for me, my father did survive, and that he went out to Africa and met my mother. I only wish he had lived long enough to meet his grandchildren and teach them his highly personalized version of Battleships.

LESLIE SCOTT *is a board game designer and the founder of Oxford Games. Scott has since devised and published more than forty games, but she is probably best known as the inventor of* Jenga, *which she self-published (as Leslie Scott Associates) and launched at the London Toy Fair in 1983.*

TICKET TO READ

Jenn Bartlett

I'm not someone who grew up with board games. As an only child, reading was my hobby, my salvation, and laid the groundwork for me to become a librarian as an adult. Games, however, were not part of my world until I married Matt in 2010. My mother purchased our very first modern board game, *Battle Cry*, a historical war game about the Civil War, for our first Christmas. We were Civil War reenactors at the time and Matt was working on his Master's in military history, so *Battle Cry* was a natural choice.

After that, we picked up some fairly simple games like *Pirates of the Spanish Main* and *Five Tribes*, but I really fell in love with games when we jumped into the complex world of *Mage Knight*. I loved how immersive it was, that it was such an involved game, and I really felt like I was wandering through all the different lands. By 2015, the epic *War of the Ring* was our favorite game, so when my husband applied to be part of the Ares Games demo team for *War of the Ring* and *Battle of Five Armies* at Gen Con I was eager to be included in this adventure.

As I was showering one day just before the trip, I thought to myself (as one often does in the shower), what if I went to Gen Con with my library business cards and tried to get a board game program going at my library? I told my director about the idea as soon as I got to work the next day, and they thought it was a great idea. So, two weeks later, we set off for Gen Con enthused for our very first board game convention.

In between teaching folks how to play *War of the Ring*, Matt and I wandered the convention floor, and I had the opportunity to speak with a variety of publishers about the new board game program I was starting, and my vision for it. Some swapped business cards with me, some offered game donations, and one, Rio Grande Games, went into their booth and pulled out three games that would become the very first games in my library's board game collection: *Dominion*, *Carcassonne: Discovery*, and *Carcassonne: The Card Game*. It was a very positive experience, and I went home feeling like my program was off to a good start.

Back at the library, I made lists of publishers to contact, watched Dice Tower Top 10 videos, scoured BoardGameGeek for the hottest games, and visited our Friendly Local Game Store (FLGS). I spent hours e-mailing, filling out "contact us" forms, and following up with publishers to see if they would be willing to donate games to my library's collection.

So, what was my idea for my library's board game program? I went into designing my board game program with some very specific purposes:

- Attract millennials.
- Be female-friendly.
- Be as open, inclusive and accessible as possible to all who wanted to play games at the library.
- Offer something different than our local FLGS.

My capstone project for my Master's in library science had focused on ways to get young adults to use the library. Young adults are often so busy with college, and training for their careers, that they don't have the time for recreational hobbies like reading, or visiting the library. I remember that when I was in college, the amount of reading I did just for myself went way down. Some people return to the library after these life changes, or when they start to have children and bring them to the library.

One of my professional goals has always been to use my library program as a method to get people to come back to the library. I'm a firm believer that when someone is passionate about something – in this case, board games – other people will feed on that energy and positivity and want to join in.

As a female in the hobby, I've experienced some, putting it mildly, interesting instances. I've had comments like "What are you here to purchase for your husband?" after entering a store. Another time, I was playing *Power Grid*, a game I had never played before, with two guys at a local store. Three-quarters through the game, they looked at each other, saw I was in the lead and said "Well, we can't let *her* win." Things like this still happen, even after thirteen years in the hobby. I knew my library program was not going to let that behavior exist.

This went hand-in-hand with point number three. Public libraries welcome everyone, no matter the person's background, how much money they have, what race, religion, gender, or sexual orientation they are. We want everyone to come and enjoy our programs, materials, and just exist in our buildings. And they must be welcome to do all of that for free, without having to purchase something. It was clear that the board gaming hobby was growing and expanding to people who had traditionally not been welcomed in some more traditional gaming spaces. It was critical to me that those people felt like they could be a part of my group.

We are lucky enough to have several friendly local game stores in my community – the Grid Games is within walking distance of the library and the Portal is just a short car ride away, and there are plenty more to choose from, too. I didn't want to duplicate what they were doing, nor did I want to try to take business away from them. Libraries and bookstores, for example, have coexisted in communities together for decades, and I wanted the same for the relationship between my library and our local game stores. Some folks are always going to want to purchase, some will purchase *and* visit the library, and some will only visit the library. I thought I could offer a program that was going to be different than our local store's Thursday evening open gaming group.

I wanted to design a program where people could come and really learn games, like they would at a convention – from someone who has already learned the game, who could teach it and bring their own copy. People wouldn't have to bring their own games, and then be disappointed if we didn't have the time to play them. I wanted participants to be able to turn up, sit at a table and relax, knowing their teacher had done the heavy lifting of learning the game, and that there was no chance of accidentally having misunderstood a rule.

There were other reasons I didn't want people to bring their own games in. My fear was that someone would come in with their precious Kickstarter-exclusive deluxe edition, worth several hundred dollars, and someone would spill coffee on it or rip a card. I didn't want people to risk their own possessions and I didn't want the library to be liable for damages. But I also wanted to make this a genuinely accessible event, regardless of participants' ability to pay for games. Tabletop gaming is a luxury hobby and not everyone is able to afford it. All librarians try to make our services as equitable as possible and requiring people to bring their own games would have been a gross mistake on our part. What if someone wanted to come but couldn't afford a game to bring? What if they came and felt bad about themselves when they saw that everyone else had expensive limited editions?

I knew that I wanted the program to partner with our local game store in some way. Libraries are often committed to supporting local businesses through programming, summer reading prizes and partnerships, so this seemed a potential win-win for both of us. I went to the game store we frequented and spoke to the manager about partnering for our monthly event. He agreed to work with us. Initially the idea was that he would be one of our regular teachers and be able to sell games at the event. Our town's library has a policy of fairness when it comes to similar businesses, so we work with as many as possible to be as equitable as possible. I approached another store near us and offered the same deal. My experience here was less than positive, as the owner said, "Why would I want to work with the library?". It was clear he saw this as something to be dismissed, not worthy, and I felt like Barney Stinson from *How I Met Your Mother* and internally said, "Challenge accepted."

Our first board game event was August 2015 and we had eighteen adults show up, a very enthusiastic group of folks. It became clear that our monthly two-and-a-half-hour session was not long enough, so we extended it to four-and-a-half hours instead. I wanted to make it work for folks who were playing longer games, or who wanted to play more than one game, and I wanted to make it worth the trip for those who had come a long distance to play. I wanted to make it very experiential: we'd make sure everyone knew what games were going to be taught, so they could get excited. Participants knew we were going to offer free snacks, and they knew they were going to have a fun and relaxing afternoon at our library.

Now we get anywhere from eighteen to forty-seven adults each time, and we've hosted local designer fairs, publisher spotlight days including Osprey, Restoration Games and Smirk & Dagger, and fostered relationships and opportunities with designers like Emerson Matsuuchi, Carl Van Ostrand, Curt Covert, Jason Miceli, and more. Building the board game community is huge for me; it's part of me giving back, encouraging designers, and bringing new gamers into the hobby.

Soon we had 135 games available for board game day and we were getting a diverse group of folks coming, mostly millennials, and regulars who were telling their friends, family and coworkers about us.

At that time, our board games were not available for the public to check out and take home. They sat in our basement stacks, only coming out during board game day. One day in summer 2017, I was, once again, in the shower (don't the best ideas come to you in the shower?!) and I thought, what if the board games circulated to the public? I had been holding them very tightly to the program but attendees had asked over and over about being able to check them out. It was time to let them be free and trust that the public would treat the games well.

I find it silly now that I had ever worried about letting the board games circulate. 135 games were cataloged, processed, and put out for the public in September 2017, and now, in May 2023, we have over one thousand board games for adults, teens and children in my library. Our circulating board games are wildly popular and we hope to have space for three thousand when we move to our new library building. To see the joy on children's faces as they pick up a game off the shelf that they want to take home and play, to see an avid hobbyist board gamer come in and be able to try a board game before they buy it, to see folks who otherwise couldn't afford to buy a board game be able to check out a game and have the exact experience as someone who could – this is where the magic happens.

I'm in a unique position as someone who is involved on the industry side as a content creator and on the professional side as a literal board game librarian. I get to talk to people on both sides about how gaming in libraries impacts the community. I've mentioned some reasons above – access, equity, inclusion – but there's so much more. Even people who love libraries often forget our ability to bring people together, to strip down barriers, and create spaces and moments for people that can literally change lives. When I'm talking to publishers about why they want to work with libraries, I remind them that there may not be a FLGS in every city, town and village in America, but there's likely to be a public library. Anyone can walk through our doors but not everyone may feel comfortable walking into a store that sells board games. I've had someone who was homeless come to several of my board game events before the pandemic. Where else would something like that happen?

Back in 2015, when I was starting out, there were fewer librarians who wanted board game programs and collections in their libraries, and publishers were often very generous with their donations. It was a great time – there were no shipping

Image: Jenn Bartlett

or manufacturing crises, product was readily available, and profit margins were, perhaps, bigger. Asking for donations is one way to start, but it is not the best method of cultivating the collection. If your library has the budget to purchase product from the companies, or by supporting their FLGS, that's a boon to both libraries and the games industry. For those libraries with slimmer budgets, try to create a strong relationship with an individual publisher, as in return for a trade discount their games can be the flagship product of the new collection.

Gaming in libraries has changed not only my job but my life. I've been able to connect with people, create new friendships, bring joy and happiness, recommend a new favorite game to play, encourage other librarians to embrace games at their libraries, break down barriers with board game publishers, help people save money, foster community and so much more.

If your local library doesn't have a board game program, ask them for it. Sometimes all it takes is for one single person to ask. Because if you're asking, there's likely to be many more in the community who also want that service or program and have just never asked. Or, if they don't have one, ask to start one and help set it up. Your local library is an amazing resource, and we welcome you.

JENN BARTLETT *is is head of Reference and Adult Services for Manchester Public Library in Connecticut, USA. She is most well-known for her segment on* The Dice Tower's *Board Game Breakfast called "From the Page to the Table." A former president of the American Library Association's GameRT, Jenn has been featured in* American Libraries *magazine, and has written for* Library Journal.

You can find Jenn on social media as The Board Game Librarian.

PLAY

PLAYING BY DESIGN

An Interview with Reiner Knizia

So, Reiner, a rather broad question, but what do board games mean to you?

Well, they have always been my hobby and now they are my job. Board games have been my life and my life would not be the same without them.

You're known as a games designer. You've said in the past that you no longer play games designed by other people to avoid having them influence your own solutions to problems you encounter. Is that right?

That's making a virtue out of a necessity. It's not that I don't want to play other people's games. I have done that much more frequently in earlier times. When I was playing other people's games, my focus was more on enjoying the games. Now I enjoy the design more.

The reality is that game design is very much playing games, playing the prototypes and making them robust, playing them with many different people. And I have the curse of so many ideas that whenever I get some victims to play games, there are always lots of my designs which are waiting for testing. So, there is never really the time or the space to play other people's games. There is always a higher priority and the greater temptation to playtest a new design.

But, as you say, there is also virtue in this because not knowing other people's solutions makes it easier to come up with new ones of your own. As soon as you know a solution, you cannot get your mind off it. If you don't know one, you're absolutely free and suddenly you find some new bridges.

Is the pleasure you get from playtesting your own designs similar to the pleasure we get from playing other people's games or would you say is it very different?

Well, that's interesting, because as a designer we could say that every game we play now is a playtest of sorts. To me, it is the same, really. It is the enjoyment of finding a set of rules where you can engage, where you have a challenge, where everybody is the same, and you can just try things out. Nothing can really go wrong – it's only a game. And it is a challenge of working within the framework of the game, and taking on the challenge and seeing how you cope with it.

I'm a mathematician, so I like to do modeling and see what you can do with the rules mechanically. So, it's really the interaction with other people which is very important for me: sitting around the table, and looking at their face when you beat them. (I'm just kidding!) For me, winning or losing is not important. And I think for most of us as players, it's not important. Of course, the *goal* of wanting to win is very important for the *game*, but who actually wins doesn't really matter.

Even if I play somebody else's game, it's kind of a playtest, because I'm experiencing what other people do. And very often I have the idea, "Oh, I would have done that differently," or "Oh, that's a really good idea, but didn't I use that already?" So, I get even more insights and "Wow!" moments when I play other people's games.

You mentioned about the interaction with other people, sitting around a table. I think that's a phrase a lot of people would use to describe the significance of games. You've designed cooperative games – notably Lord of the Rings *– which we think of as fundamentally different to competitive games because people aren't playing against one another. How do you see the interaction in a cooperative game? Is it very different?*

For me, the situation of sitting around the table with other people is the important one, and that doesn't change if you play competitively or cooperatively. I think I almost prefer the cooperative game because you can win together. Winning is not important, but if we play against each other, one has to win, one has to lose, and I have to act against you. The experience becomes even more rewarding and people come together even more, so the common experience is even deeper when you play a cooperative game and try to help each other.

Whoowasit? – a cooperative game with electronics inside – is our most successful game ever. It won the Kinderspiel (Children's Game of the Year Award, in Germany) and sold a huge number of copies. It's very funny. I meet people these days in their twenties and thirties and they say, "I grew up with *Whoowasit?* and now my kids play it," and so on. This is very rewarding feedback. So, I think, if I have a choice, I prefer a very good cooperative game – but they are rare. That's the problem.

Yes, Whoowasit? *is a hybrid game – it has an electronic component – which is another aspect that slightly changes the nature of board games. How do you feel that affects the experience of playing the game and the interaction between players?*

Games are a mirror of our time. And the games twenty, fifty years ago are different to the games today. The speed of the game people expect today, the dynamics – you would never get through a chess game. It's slow and nothing happens. It's like in the movies. If nobody is dead in the first minute, the movie is boring. Look at *Casablanca*, look at the old movies. It's very different. So, as times change, the type of game really changes. And, as a mirror of our world, clearly everywhere you look there are electronics. Even the washing machine has electronics. So, it's quite clear that the digital world must also come into our games.

But there is the other aspect of digital gaming – over networks and so on. That's quite different. I don't mind if I have a printed board or if I roll out a screen and upload a board. I actually enjoy it if the board then gives some atmospheric sounds and does something. If you look at *Whoowasit?*, the talking chest (which is electronic) doesn't take you away from playing the game together – it actually enhances it. It helps, of course, with the cooperative nature of the game, because the enemy is in the box. So, in this case, the digital aspects enhance the board game, but it's still a social board game.

You've also designed solo games, like Brains. *I actually just noticed that on the cover of my copy the icon for the number of players is two people even though it's a solo game. It's interesting how much we see games as implicitly social, but there are also solo games.*

This is a very interesting point you're raising and it's also a very up-to-date topic for me. It depends what you call a solo game. I think solo games, maybe because of the pandemic, have become more popular and publishers are keen to have a variant on their normal social games which you can play by yourself. So, it's not two to four players but *one* to four players. There are good solutions and there are some dumb solutions.

We can simply have a dummy player and you have to play for this dummy player in kind of an algorithm. But if I want to play a solo game, I don't want to play my counterpart for it. What's the point? It's not elegant. For me, that's non-innovative and it's poor design. (I'm hopefully not insulting too many people!)

But there are different types of solo game. If you look at a card game like Klondike or Patience, this is solitaire play. Another type, like you mentioned, is *Brains*, the whole line there, which I did with Pegasus. This is more like a logic puzzle – I wouldn't really call these social, one-player games. They're more of a logical challenge to be solved in many levels. So, this is more a brain exercise game – hence it's called *Brains*. I wouldn't really call it – from the heart – a solo game, a single-player game.

I've always dreamed of saying, "Can we not do one-player games which are, in inverted commas, 'real games' – games that feel like social games, but just for one player." And I have just created – and it was announced at the Nuremberg Toy Fair – a line of single-player games, with Schmidt. They are called *For One*, and these are really games which are only playable for one player, but they feel like a normal social board or card game. So, you don't have a counter-player, but nevertheless it feels like you take your turn and you do something, and then you take your next turn and your next turn. So, essentially you take one turn after another, there is no real counter-player, but you're still playing in an environment, you're exploring things – you're deciphering in Egypt, for example. To me, that was my ambition – to create something where I have a real solo game, a game for one player. The jury will be out there to judge, but that was my ambition and I'm happy with what I created, so now people can see if they are happy with it.

I think it is very apparent that, as you say, there's a line of solo games that are adaptations of multiplayer games – which is probably a necessity – and there's a line of puzzles. It's very interesting that you think there is a space in the middle, for a solo game which feels like a social game. With a multiplayer game, as a designer, you can gauge the social interaction from the people you playtest with. How do you playtest a solo game to see if it is rewarding a player in that way?

In a way, very simply. I design it – and, of course, the designing and playing is together, so in this case I can do it by myself.

Once I had agreed with Schmidt that I would design *For One*, I actually booked two-and-a-half weeks away from the office. I just locked myself in a room and designed and played and worked on these games. I can get quite far by myself and come to a first, playable version. Then I would give the package with the rules to the playtesters around me, and they would play it themselves, and they would write down how much time they need for the individual game, and they would also give detailed feedback.

The games we're talking about have around twenty levels, so the challenges which the game brings you vary. I think that's also important because counter-players, of course, make the game much more varied than is possible in a one-player game. So, the single player gets twenty scenarios to play or fifteen scenarios to play. The playtesters would play it by themselves and they would give me feedback: "This one I liked, this one was too difficult, this one was too easy, this one was just boring..." We have a lot of scenarios, so we put them into chapters and say, "Okay, these five build nicely on top of one another." Then there's the rules, of course, which build a little bit on top of each other with each chapter, so then we have the next chapter with a few games, and that's how it comes together.

You mentioned earlier that people have told you that they grew up playing your games and now they play them with their children. A lot of those people will also now play some of your other games as adults – you've designed games for both – which leads on to the question of audience. How does your intended audience factor into your designs?

You have to accept that you can never please all of the people. This is, I think, the big challenge when publishers become an international company and then try to satisfy all markets at the same time. You sink the game down to the smallest common denominator and you lose a lot. Games are culture so if you try to be everything to everybody, you end up being nothing to anybody.

This was a little bit of a challenge to me in the 90s, because people put me in the box of these big tile-laying games and big strategy games and people got disappointed with some of my other games because they said, "Oh, that's not as good as

Tigris & Euphrates." Well, it was a different direction. I think people have now accepted that I do different types of games. I may set out with a certain audience in mind, but if I start out with a specific type of game in mind and then the game develops and the game wants to go somewhere else, I'm not forcing it to stay where it is. What I want to have is the most excellent game I can create. And once the game is finished, then I will determine what is the right target group. I mean, I make sure that there is a target group, yes, but what is the right target group for this game? Who is the right publisher who can reach the target group and can do this game justice? And, then, hopefully by having it in the right product line or in the right box, people will recognize what type of game it is. It's very important. You have a cover. If the cover looks too young, or too old, then you lose people. And, of course, the price and the box size and so on also establish expectations. So, there's a lot of aspects which can subtly communicate what type of game that is.

Image: Marcus Schlaf

But the game meanders as it develops. For me games are like children. You cannot force them somewhere. You can only try to help them develop their own strengths. As a little example, when I designed *Ra*, that was just after I retired from my banking job and became a full-time designer. I had lots of time, because the business pressures were not there yet. I started out with the idea of having a big board – it was set in Egypt already – and we would have a little card game, we'd play a ten-minute card game, and then we would try to win some cards. And if I win a pyramid card, I could build a pyramid. And if I win a Pharaoh card, I could do something in the Pharaoh side. And then I had a fertility card. And I could do a boat on the river and so on. And once you had played out these things for another five minutes, we played the next card game. And we played that, and it lasted about three to four hours. It was far too long. So, I really went back and said, "What is really innovative about this?" I came to the conclusion that it is actually the card game, where you collect the stuff, and we don't need the big board. So, I said, "Okay, we'll do the cards." We laid out the cards in front of us – and now, when everybody lays out the cards in front of them, it takes up too much space. Suddenly, it's no longer cards, it's tiles. Then you need a different distribution mechanism. And then we came up the little board where you put the tiles out, and you bid for them with the suns.

So, that's just a little example of how much a game can change. And it's funny – I mean, maybe the original design, it still sounds interesting to me, having a big board and playing little card games in it – but that's not how it went. As long as there's a good game coming out of it – and *Ra* is a nice game – it's fine. With *Ra*, what fascinates me as an innovation is that it's an auction game in its heart. Yes, it's a civilization-building game, but not really – it's an auction game. But you're not only auctioning for the goodies with which you build your civilization, you're also auctioning for your future auction power – because you auction with the suns, of different values, and if you have the highest bid, you put it in the middle, and then it stays in the middle, and the next auction will also auction not only the tiles which come out, but also the sun. Suddenly, people realize if there is the highest sun there because the last player wanted all these tiles, I could actually bid without having tiles there because I just go for the bidding power. So, this is a really nice variation – that you have to balance between something that is wanted now or powerful later.

What do you hope people get out of it when they sit down to play one of your games?

Enjoyment and stimulation and a good time with each other. I mean, our motto on business cards and letterheads and everything is "Bringing enjoyment to the people." This was a motto I created a long time ago when I started the business and I asked myself what it really is that I need to deliver. The motto "I want to make money," is not only not true, it's also self-defeating. The aim is really to bring enjoyment to people. And if people have a good time with the games, they will play the games. This is the only reason they play them. It's a leisure time activity, we are not forcing them. So, if they have a good time, if they enjoy it, if they feel stimulated by it, if it's attractive, if they see that their kids or their friends like it, that's the biggest reward.

DR REINER KNIZIA *is one of the world's most successful and prolific board game designers, having designed over seven hundred published games. Reiner's game Keltis was awarded the Spiel des Jahres (Game of the Year) award in 2008. His Lord of the Rings board game (2000) is credited with beginning the popular revival of cooperative games, among his many other achievements.*

Reiner Knizia was talking to Matt Keefe. You can find Reiner at knizia.de

CONNECTIONS

Holly Nielsen

As a kid I remember wanting to play board games with my family, which did happen but not with as much frequency as I would have liked. The *Disney Trivial Pursuit* box sat up on the shelf gathering dust most of the time. My mum worked long hours so finding the time to sit down with all of us was tricky. I remember reaching up to where it sat on the shelf and bringing it down on my own. I would get out the board and read through the cards, making myself feel very smart because of course I knew that Ariel's crab friend was called Sebastian. Pfft, try harder next time, game. The best part though was the pieces. I was always the pink playing piece, my dad was blue, mum was yellow, and my brother was green. Pouring out the little pie sections from the plastic bag they were kept in and slotting them into place in pleasing colorful arrangements was a favorite pastime of mine as a kid when no one was around to play. I realize this picture I'm painting could be seen as quite sad. A kid playing with a board game on their own and hoping they'd get to play it with people soon. But doing this didn't make me feel particularly lonely. It reinforced my love of the times my family did all sit down together to play.

This is something I have learned through years of researching the history of board games and the play that happened with them. When people talk about board games, they often talk about connections. Connections with other people, connections they make to the past through nostalgia and memories, connections to the present with how these experiences were formative. Even this experience in my own childhood is saying a lot about my connections to others and my relationship to them, and how I related them to this game. Beyond these personal connections, my work as a historian specializing in play and board games has meant that games have become a conduit for how I connect ideas to the past, and how the past connects to the present. They can seem an unassuming object, but their presence has shaped my life.

Connections to the Present

Near the end of my undergraduate degree, I took a module that involved us going to the Black Cultural Archives in London to look at some materials held in their collections. At the time, I was twenty-one and had been working in videogame journalism for about two years alongside my degree. This was 2015, a particularly bad time to be a female videogame journalist. Online hate campaigns were raging against women and minorities about our presence in the space. I received threats for doing my job. I had colleagues who received far worse and left the space entirely. A lot of this venom was sent under the thin excuse of "keeping politics out of games." It was not a good time, to put it absurdly mildly.

As a history student interested in material culture, I was very aware that everything is political, and subject to its social and cultural contexts. But that visit to the Black Cultural Archives put my life on a track I couldn't have predicted. One of the items shown to us was a homemade board game from the 1970s titled *Womanopoly*. It was made by Stella Dadzie, a hugely influential activist and educator in the Black British women's movement. The whole point of the game is that one person plays as a man, the other as a woman, and the person playing as a woman will always lose, because of society's unequal treatment and structural misogyny. Looking at this game was like being snapped awake.

This game created as a form of protest led me to start looking up other games made for this purpose, including board games published by the Suffragettes in early twentieth-century Britain. They confirmed what I knew but couldn't point to at the time. Games and play had not only always been political, they were part of political protest. From there I never really looked back. The more I researched, the more I found how even the most mundane everyday games told us a great deal about the society and culture of which they were a product. This research collided with my desire to show a longer history of games and play that explored these themes, the result of which was an MPhil written on the commercial, social and cultural history of British board games from 1880 to 1939. Though this research was fulfilling, I felt there was something missing. I was covering the games themselves, but I lacked the actual play that happened with them – a much harder, more ephemeral thing to try to capture and analyze. This would turn into my PhD research. To try and locate the play that happened with board games, I turned to oral history interviews done during the 1960s. Board games feature in over half of all the interviews in what is a very expansive dataset. But more interestingly for me, whenever board games were brought up, what they were often really talking about was the people they played them with. People remembered moments such as deliberately letting their mother win at Snakes and Ladders so they could see her smile, sibling arguments over Ludo, and fathers so enthralled by chess it caused tension in the home.

Board games captivated me as a researcher as they became conduits through which to explore larger themes. Whether it was the big questions about the politics of gender and imperialism, down to the politics of everyday interactions between family members. They are not just interesting objects on their own but a starting point for so many potential questions. So, there's a whole plethora of reasons why I landed on board games as my chosen subject for my historical research. One of the main ones is that I'm interested in people and their connections to one another. Learning about the everyday lives and interpersonal connections of those that lived before us is deceptively hard. History is dominated by the unique, the big event, the ground-breaking movements. But, beneath all this is the everyday and the mundane. The routine lives of the vast majority that make up the past.

Connections to the Past

My research, then, has been dominated by games that to the outside world may seem quite boring, or at least not fun to play. Ludo and Snakes and Ladders are the dominant games of my research, with chess and draughts (known elsewhere as checkers) a little way beneath them in terms of direct mentions. Simple roll-and-move board games have been dismissed in the past by researchers because they take no skill to play. But it is their ubiquity and their incredibly low bar for participation that makes them interesting. I've seen more Ludo, Snakes and Ladders, and simple roll-and-move boards than any one person should probably ever have to see, but I still think the history around them is fascinating.

Because I'm a historian who looks at board games and play, I often deal with childhoods and people remembering their childhoods, often a very emotionally charged thing. But two particular moments stand out to me. One of these was on a game's board itself. *The Prince's Quest* was published by Roberts Brothers around 1910. It's a simple roll-and-move board game with a fairytale theme. At some point, one copy of this game was in the possession of a child called Joan; we know this because she wrote her name in very large letters on the back of the board. This game set had playing pieces in the form of cardboard princes to represent the players on the board. Joan had written "Mother" on both sides of one of the pieces, and "Father" on both sides of another. Could these have been her parents' playing pieces when they played with her? Did Joan associate these pieces with her parents? Of course, it is impossible to know with so little evidence. But what we do know is that Joan brought to this game her own personal layer of meaning, one not found in the rules. I remembered the *Disney Trivial Pursuit* pieces I had as a child. Yellow was Mum's piece, blue was Dad's.

Another moment that really stuck with me was a letter sent by Donald Miller to the *Lowestoft Journal*, published on June 4, 1910, answering a question about favorite games by stating that Snakes and Ladders was his: "I think it is a very nice game, and a lot of people like to play it." He continued, "I very often get father and mother to have a game with me, as I am not fortunate enough to have any brothers or sisters." It's a simple letter, but its earnestness and the simplicity of a child enjoying playing a board game with his parents (and slightly lamenting the lack of others to play with), is so universal that I remember it often. Both things – the fairytale board game and pieces with the pencil writing of a child on them, and the letter from the boy who loved Snakes and Ladders – immediately take me back to my own childhood. The fine thread of recognition and emotion across time still tugs at my heart.

Connections to One Another

Studying the role that board games played in the lives and relationships of those who lived a century ago inevitably leads me to reflect on my own experiences. My childhood did not involve as much board game play as perhaps I would have liked. But there are particular games that I can't help but associate with certain people. Draughts is one of those. I remember being sat in the living room of my parents' house, concentrating hard in an effort to win a game against my grandad. He was principled to a fault and had spent his life serving others as a Methodist minister. The generational divide between us felt wider than it was in reality. There wasn't a lot we could find common ground in. A love of history was one thing we both shared, as was walking in the countryside. But despite our love and respect for one another, there was a distance. However, this would disappear when playing draughts.

Draughts was a level playing field, simple enough for me as a child to understand, complex enough to keep us both entertained. It felt that we were from entirely different worlds at times, but the draughts board provided a mutual meeting ground. Imaginative play can be difficult to engage in as an adult, let alone as an adult with very few shared reference points with the child. The rules of draughts took away the responsibility of creating a shared playful language and gave us one we both felt comfortable in. It allowed us to enjoy one another's company without pressure or social anxiety. He would often say that he would one day teach me how to play chess. Unfortunately, he never had the chance. But to this day when I see a draughts or chess board, I think of him.

Trivial Pursuit also comes back in this area of my life. From *Disney Trivial Pursuit* with my family, to later experiences, it has become an oddly, unexpectedly formative game. When I was a graduate student at Cambridge, I remember one evening of bonding with my fellow historians playing the game after a couple of pints, and I've never before or since seen anything quite like the fear in the eyes of a group of historians when they had to answer a history question in *Trivial Pursuit*. A couple of years later I would find myself in a bar with my partner and making ourselves laugh to the point of headache by looking through the question cards for a truly cursed edition of the game called *Trivial Pursuit Baby Boomer Edition, which* we'd found in the corner of the bar. If you said "The Beatles!" in response to any question, I'm pretty sure you had a seventy percent chance of being correct.

As well as connections to the past and connecting the past to the present, board games have allowed me to connect with family, friends and loved ones. I'm sure this will ring true for many people. Spending time together enjoying one another's company over something that enables us to be playful, silly, and joyous is a powerful thing that should not be underestimated. As you grow older you seem to have fewer and fewer chances to be playful. Society is uneasy with adults playing in many ways. When I tell people about my research, it's telling that the assumption is that I must look at children and childhood, when that is only one aspect of play. In fact, it was difficult finding an institution that would let me do my PhD research and not put me in the box of "history of childhood" or "childhood studies." Board games are a site of playfulness for all ages, and for intergenerational interaction, and they have been for centuries. They have provided me with profound connections both to those directly around me and those who lived centuries ago.

HOLLY NIELSEN *is a historian, writer and narrative designer based in London. She is a PhD candidate at Royal Holloway, University of London, where she researches the history of British board games and play. She has written about games and play for a number of publications including* The Guardian *and the* New Statesman. *She also works as a writer and narrative designer for video games.*

GAMES MAKE MEMORIES

Jack Doddy

When I was twelve, I went to stay with my brother in his university student house for three days, surviving entirely on fizzy drinks and pizza. My brother, who was the progenitor of all my nerdy loves, took me along to the university sci-fi and fantasy society's weekly board game night. This was important not just because it was fun and nerdy but because it was an excuse to see and spend time with my brother, which I hadn't done since he moved away to study. This change had been pretty tough for me, since he was one of the few people that understood all the nerdy things I liked.

I was apparently an adorable little child, sitting with these young adults, playing games for hours. From what I can recall, the group enjoyed the novelty of such a little kid trying his hand at these big games. Perhaps they actually just found it annoying and were being polite to the little brother of one of their members… Either way, I had a lot of fun. I had played *Monopoly* and *Trivial Pursuit* and the like with our family, but this was my first time playing more specialist, hobby board games like *CATAN*, *Betrayal at the House on the Hill* and *The Werewolves of Millers Hollow*. Oh, and *Talisman*[1] – I played it first there and became obsessed. So obsessed that every birthday and Christmas for the next few years I got some sort of expansion for it. Whenever my father travelled, he would stop in any little hobby shop he could find to see if he could get some *Talisman* box I hadn't got yet. Even when the man went to the tiny island of Jersey, he managed to find the one board game shop and magicked up a copy of *The Reaper* expansion for *Talisman*.

I have an incredibly vivid memory of playing the hidden-role game *The Resistance* at my brother's board game night. *The Resistance* is a game in which the good guys try to succeed at missions by picking a team and the secret bad guys try to sabotage them by sneaking onto the roster. I was one of the bad guys. It was the last round, and the score was tied. I had convinced the table to bring me on the final mission and I was on track to win, when I just… let them succeed. The good team cheered; the rest of the villains looked at me with a "What the hell?!" stare, and I said, "But they trusted me…" Little old me hadn't quite grasped the concept of being a baddie yet.

I brought this passion home with me, and I am extremely thankful that I did, because the love of these board games, and

---

1 *Talisman* is a massive adventure game that takes hours to play. It also takes up an entire dining room table. The expansions only compound these two facts and the number of expansions that I had slammed into my edition meant that everyone came to dread the set up and play time.

general nerdery, has kept my friends and me in each other's lives. For the seven years since leaving school, our chats have been dominated by gaming talk – reminiscing on previous games, plotting next sessions and me getting excited about whatever ridiculously massive game I had picked up that month. "Hey look, this one came with a dragon!"

Because I'd been playing these kinds of games for a bit longer than most of my friends, I had a better understanding of dice games and their tactics when we first started these gaming sessions together. *Risk*[2] is a game that my friends and I keep coming back to. For us, *Risk* has a *Monopoly*-like power for making and breaking friendships. You learn which of your friends are backstabbing monsters and should never be trusted with world domination. When we began playing *Risk* together, they knew that I had more experience with these sorts of games, so they would almost always immediately work together to murder me as quickly as possible. In *Risk*, this means I would usually blockade Oceania and wait them out, because I know my friends well enough to know that their patience and loyalty to any alliance would run out quickly. I remember two of my friends, Olly and Tom, entering a peaceful alliance until they rooted me out of my Australian bunker. Tom was much happier about the arrangement than Olly. As I watched Tom, I noticed that he started to sweat, and his face slowly turned red. He stared at the table in an attempt to contain his excitement. He promised, repeatedly, that he would never betray his ally...

---

2   In particular, we enjoy *Risk: Legacy*, a version where all the players sign the board, and it changes as you play, naming continents and cities. This is perfect for us as it encourages us to play regularly to unlock all its secrets. It's also why Australia is the capital of the world and the rest is covered in ruins and nuclear wastelands. I played the long game.

and Olly begrudgingly accepted this. As Tom's turn drew nearer, he started to shake with anticipation. As soon as it was his turn, he leapt up and slammed every troop he had on Olly's undefended border, and he surged through his former ally's continent. The rest of the table, to this day, do not trust Tom in any competitive game. We watched him lie remorselessly, and he continues to do this in every head-to-head game we play. Not only do we love him for it but I am quite happy to not be the first and main target for everyone in these games anymore. And that's the weird magic of board games – it's rare that you will ever look back fondly on the memory of your friends lying through their teeth in any other context.

I will hold on to these little memories and look back fondly on them for the rest of my life. I will probably end up bringing up one of these stories at Tom's wedding, when I inevitably warn his bride never to trust him in a board game for their entire marriage. This is what good board games and friends do. They make memories.

JACK DODDY *is a British publishing assistant who chooses to live perpetually in games and novels. From sci-fi to fantasy, from tabletop to video, it's all fine as long as he doesn't have to acknowledge reality. He is also a regular in the competitive wargaming scene. This is his first published piece.*

BOARD GAMES ARE A STORY, NOT A DESTINATION

Allen Stroud

Picture the scene. Old school friends reunite for a weekend game. A large box is brought to the dining room table, the contents unpacked and set out according to the instructions. Colored plastic counters, cardboard tiles, stacks of cards and trays are all arranged and organized.

The friends take their seats, and for the rest of the evening they do battle in an asymmetric war. Cards, counters and pieces on the table are exchanged. They represent the ebbs and falls of empires, intergalactic wars, sprawling corporations or feuding nations. Happy hours are spent together, chatting, scheming, laughing and enjoying the competitive conflict.

I have always loved board games. From my first games of *Monopoly* and *Risk*, to *Axis and Allies*, *Game of Thrones* and *Twilight Imperium*, I have shared experiences with other players who become allies and enemies over the board, but who always remain friends when it's put away.

If I think back to those first games, my best memories of them are of when I was playing them without other people. Many game designers are not fans of *Monopoly*. When families gather and pull out their battered copy to play on a holiday afternoon, the game gradually devolves into a drawn-out, inevitable defeat for all but one of the players. However, I played *Monopoly* on my own for days. I was all of the players; I rewrote the rules to tell a story of the twists and turns of financial booms and crashes. My tokens risked everything and turned sinking debt into roaring profit. Then I put the game away and went on to something else.

With *Risk*, my armies had leaders and stories. I took an atlas and started to add detail to the game board with pencils and pens. My family and friends didn't understand why I felt the need to elaborate and embellish the games but for me it was a natural thing to do to flesh out the story of the game. Empires needed to trade, so out came the *Monopoly* money to be used as currency. I invented commodities and turned the world into a peaceful place. Nations at war became allies. The story of a world divided by conflict and brought together by trade became a fictional history all of its own.

The first games I played with my friends where the narrative felt like it was part of the experience were *Shogun* and *Axis and Allies*. The historical context brought meaning to the game. The different elements of production and combat made each game turn a story in itself. Don't get me wrong, I wanted to win – I always want to win – but as the games progressed, I found I didn't mind losing, particularly if the experience ebbed and flowed, with everyone getting drawn into what might happen.

Over time, I played more and more board games. Some of these were collaborative, some competitive. Many involved chance, with dice rolls dictating the speed and outcome of key challenges. These moments drew out a different kind of story – destiny, or the luck of the gods interfering with the decisions of each player. A low score became a tragedy, or a lucky roll meant that the outcome was fated to happen.

A game I played frequently is the legendary fantasy board game *Talisman*, originally produced by Games Workshop in 1983. *Talisman* is a little like Snakes and Ladders, in that in both games, dice are rolled to determine pieces' movements. However, in *Talisman* the addition of cards, challenges and direct player-versus-player elements, along with a powerful fantasy theme, adds to the simple premise of simply trying to get from the start to the end. This is a fantasy quest made real, a competition to defeat the monster who lies in wait for the first player who reaches their lair. You really had to figure out how to use the dice and other random elements to your advantage.

The flat cardboard tiles and colorful character cards of *Kingmaker* from Avalon Hill told me, as a teenager, the story of the Wars of the Roses, introducing me to a historical period that hadn't been covered in history class. The Earl of Warwick, Henry Hotspur and the failing King Henry VI were characters I could read about as we played. *Kingmaker* gave me the opportunity to rewrite their story, to save the nation for the Lancastrians by putting down the Yorkist rebellion before it started.

Game after game of *Kingmaker* taught me that there is a fundamental element to any victory in a competitive multiplayer boardgame – the participation of all the other players. None of us get to win unless someone else loses. Competitive play with friends is a safe environment in which to experience losing.

Evaluating the experience, and still taking positives from it is an important part of adult life. In some respects, losing to a friend allows the sting of defeat to be lessened. Most of the time, the relationship means more than how many territories my friend captured in *Risk*, although I am sure there are exceptions to the rule. The story of the game experience itself also cushions the blow of any loss. You have shared something with the people participating in the boardgame – these are the only people who will know how close you came to victory in those last despairing moments.

In *Kingmaker*, as with *Monopoly*, the experience gradually narrows. Players are eliminated and left to sit on the sidelines as the finale plays out, an experience that I always found to be awkward. I never considered until I was much older that this was a flaw in the design. Better designs incorporate defeat into the story. I've played many games of *Battlestar Galactica* and *Dead of Winter*. There are challenges to overcome and traitors in your midst. Failure can be victory for those players tasked to make the world burn. But that doesn't make the game any less enjoyable. Next time, the situation will be different, and we'll figure out who to put out of the airlock before they sabotage the ship.

The majority of board game experiences are moments we share with people we know. The game is a vehicle for spending time with people we care about. The connections between people are what shapes the event. Friends and family know each other well, which helps when plotting the demise of your enemies on the board, but these are never enemies in person. For a few hours, you are all participating in a story together, one created by the activity of assembling and moving counters, exchanging pieces and discovering new parts of the game.

A gaming evening will ebb and flow. Sometimes the play can be the focus of attention, sometimes catching up on what has been going on in the real lives of your friends is more important. A good board game incorporates this into the experience. Game turns or phases provide an opportunity to make the time for socializing and catching up while ordering pizza, or taking a break for a drink. These activities are part of the evening you share with friends. They also let you discuss the story of the game and imagine the moments from the perspective of your soldiers or your starship commanders. In games like *Twilight Imperium* or *Eclipse: Second Dawn for the Galaxy*, hundreds of imaginary lives are placed in danger as soon as you move your counters onto another tile. Spare a thought for the technicians, engineers and marines onboard those ships!

In a cooperative boardgame like *Arkham Horror*, the objective is shared. The players control investigator characters, exploring the city of Arkham as supernatural horror rips through the walls between worlds. The investigators coordinate their efforts, but each works alone, trying to defend our world from an existential demonic threat. While this is not a player vs player game, the enemy is formidable. Every time I play brings forth a different story of how the characters either achieve victory or are obliterated by godlike entities – a tale of glorious triumph or tragic defeat. The monstrous enemies of the game's Cthulhu mythos linger in my imagination long after they have been defeated on the board.

My favorite epic boardgame experience is *Twilight Imperium*. The third and fourth editions of the game are weekend-long space operas that build a vast sprawling galactic narrative as civilizations fight for control of an interstellar empire. This is a science fiction boardgame with all the requisite elements. I find that the rich fiction and visuals presented on the box, in the manual, and on all of the playing pieces of a board game inspire me to really imagine the story that emerges as we play. The material is all part of the presentation and becomes a catalyst for my imagination. I will never be a galactic fleet commander, or a medieval general leading a rebellion against other factions after the death of the king, but these fictional worlds linger and haunt my dreams, and the imagery on the game becomes a guide to seeing them when I close my eyes.

Game publishers have provided fuel for this imaginative drive. No longer are *Star Wars* and *Star Trek* the sole sources of science fiction imagery, nor are *Lord of the Rings* and *Dungeons & Dragons* the only places to go for fantasy. Books, computer games and television series set in the worlds of board games all add to the existing narratives of specific fictional worlds, connecting the game state with a much larger narrative that I (along with the other thousands of players, viewers and readers) can participate in.

All of this adds to the context of the game on the table. The more I know about The Argent Flight of *Twilight Imperium*, the more I can imagine the tense conversations on board their battlefleets as they prepare a last-ditch defense against overwhelming odds. I might be praying for fortunate dice rolls against a friend who will have more dice than me, but the crew of each ship are placing their trust in comrades and commanders to outwit and outfox the enemy. They are hoping that the scientists from laboratories on their home world have done good work, and that they will find their weapons effective against the invading ships. Only I know how I mucked up my research strategy and that I now need to roll really well to hit!

The moment when all the stratagems are revealed is where all the players come together to witness defeat and victory. There is always more of the former than the latter. Participation is required for there to be a moment of appreciation. There are laurels for the winners, but also an acknowledgment that winning means a lot less than the time shared in the contest.

A good boardgame lets even the defeated walk away with a positive experience and the desire to play again. Lessons are learned, stories have been told and plans will be revised when the plastic space empires are resurrected for another showdown among friends on a regular gaming night.

We have come a long way from *Monopoly* with the family once a year. These days, there are many options competing to be your boardgame of choice for a particular social occasion with family or friends, or family *and* friends. The theme you choose, the adventure you decide upon, could be one of many. You may want to stick to a cooperative experience, a safe opportunity for the players to work together against a common threat, but spare a thought for the visceral emotional rollercoaster of the competitive, player vs player boardgame, and the poignant cutting experience of a powerful, tragic defeat.

So, we come to the end. The old friends are done. The table battleground has become a wasteland of scorched earth. Enemies lie defeated, to the victor go the spoils. The world is saved or doomed based on the dice, cards and decisions made between slices of pizza, sweets and beer (for those not driving home).

DR ALLEN STROUD *is a lecturer and researcher at Coventry University in the UK. He runs the Creative Futures research project with the Defence Science and Technology Laboratory (DSTL), a conversation between science fiction writers and government experts on what challenges we will face in the future. Stroud is also Chair of the British Science Fiction Association.*

Find out more about Allen and his work at www.allenstroud.com

BRAIN GAMES

Lynn Potyen

It was never my plan to own a business.

When my son Erik was a preschooler, he was diagnosed with a speech delay. As a young mom, I thought the blame landed on my shoulders. I hadn't seen that he was behind until his younger sister, Rachel, began interpreting for him. After the diagnosis, I was afraid that Erik would lag behind his friends, and that his limited communication skills might lead to him being shunned by his peers.

Erik began attending speech therapy sessions, where his therapist would have him play board games so he could model multiple syllable words, which he avoided saying. These games were American-style games that focus largely on dice and luck. The therapist wanted us to take games home and work on lessons, but it felt to me like Erik would only play games with the therapist as if he was "performing" for her, rather than out of enjoyment.

That next summer, in the August of 2000, my husband and I attended Gen Con in Milwaukee, a large game convention. I stumbled upon a game company called Playroom Entertainment, where I was introduced to European-style children's games. I realized that these games offered a very different experience, one paved with choices, not just rolling dice and hoping for good luck. I purchased four of their titles: *Sherlock*, *Catch the Match*, Papa Bear, and Right Turn, Left Turn. Erik was instantly enthralled, he loved to play; he loved this new challenge. He was finally in control of his destiny and began wanting to play more. The game became a vehicle he could focus on as he played, removing the pressure from him, and his speech improved.

The main difference between the games his speech therapist had introduced and the ones we were now enjoying at home were the mechanics of the games. After that, at our speech therapy sessions, I focused on listening to what the therapist was trying to teach Erik, rather than the games she chose to play with him, and adapted the games at home to match her lessons. I learned a lot in those sessions. I began to see how to manipulate games to fit the intended lesson by changing the choices and manipulating the mechanics.

Over the course of the next five years, I was telling people about games they didn't know existed and encouraging Erik's teachers and classmates to play in school. Without realizing it, I was building a community of people. Eventually my husband suggested that I open a game store. I was reluctant and to be honest the idea scared me. I had a job at the elementary school that paid well and I enjoyed quite a lot. It was only when my family encouraged me that I took the next leap. In October of

2006, I opened the doors to my new store, The GameBoard, where I focused on brain health.

Though I had realized early on in my work with Erik that tabletop games helped with learning disabilities, now I was able to see the connection to overcoming social situations, autism, and helping senior citizens as they aged. By building relationships with our local libraries, schools, chamber of commerce, dementia network, cancer care community and adult rehab facilities, I was able to help people learn and communicate through games. This drove our store mission to focus on games to help with education, dementia, and occupational and social therapy.

Games have helped members of our community with memory loss make new memories, families with learning disabilities build bridges, people with physical issues refine movement techniques, and individuals who were lonely have made friends. Games have been a vehicle to help individuals succeed in areas where they previously struggled. By taking a game and moving the focus off the individual and onto the object of play, I have been able to open their minds and remove fear and other barriers.

When working with students, I started by adapting rules of various games, changing the speed of gameplay and working with games that had a short play time. Speed-based games are great for helping students build better response times and improve hand–eye coordination. I adapted speed games like *Spot it*, *Jungle Speed*, *Taco Cat Goat Cheese Pizza* and *Rainbow Rabbits* by giving the faster student a two or three second penalty, so that the other players can proceed without stress and worry. Children who excel in sports are often very good in these areas, but children who are less confident in their physical talents sometimes shy away from games that depend on quick reasoning or swift responses. I always explain the added time by reminding the faster student that they want everyone to succeed, and the game will be better if they allow the slower player to proceed at their own speed. This gives both students a chance to grow (one in social kindness and the other in processing) and eventually both students become better challengers. Children typically want everyone to be involved. By cultivating empathy in the students toward each other, they learn to give each other space to grow and achieve together, and build better relationships.

Playing against someone purely in order to beat them doesn't make for good memories, often leaving one person happy and everyone else determined to not participate again. I remember playing arcade-style video games with my neighbors as I was growing up. It was the early 80s, and I didn't have a computer console to play on at home, so my only chance was playing at their house. We would take turns and when it came to my turn, I would fail in about thirty seconds after trying to climb a ladder or jump over a monster. I would ask for practice time, and they would tell me that this *was* practice time. I was humiliated at my inability to play at their level and frustrated at my lack of skill. When we played board games, I could slow down my turn and deeply think over what my move would be. It didn't necessarily mean that I would win, but I felt better at my ability to understand the situation and process the activity.

By playing together against the game, players learn to respect the strengths of the other individuals. Often, I saw that the students who excelled at speed games are the slower players in these cooperative games. By giving the other students a chance to shine, they learn grace and kindness toward the other players. By staggering speed-based and cooperative games in a classroom session, students start to see strengths and weaknesses and help each other to strive and have fun. I enjoy using *Castle Panic, Forbidden Island, Exit* games, *5 Minute Dungeon, 5 Minute Mystery, The Mind, Harry Potter Hogwarts Battle,* or *Similo* depending on the age of the players and the time constraints of the setting.

Games that are strictly "learning games" often fall flat because the game play usually isn't very engaging. It's important to find something the participants really want to play. I call this the "crave." Finding games that stimulate kids to be cooperative, engaged, competitive and energized builds a craving for the next game. It gets kids to want to improve themselves, not to learn for a teacher but to learn skills that they need to be better people and lifelong learners.

Neuroatypical learners are more common than you would expect; people all learn differently. Our strengths, challenges and adaptations are not weaknesses but a quilt of learning styles. Games help figure out what paths are available and challenge us to try something that is outside our comfort zone with little penalty. In my experience, some individuals on the autistic spectrum have natural strengths in resource-acquiring games. Games like *7 Wonders, Terraforming Mars,* or *Great Western Trail* (where you are buying and selling goods, building colonies in outer space, or following historical story lines) might be of deep interest to a person with learning abilities different from others. This is a way to interact and learn about a subject. It's sometimes hard to learn about something that has no substance or connection and games are a vehicle to bridge that.

A few years after we'd opened, I was working with an older couple at a SPARK program for people with dementia and their caregivers. The wife was dealing with the later stages of dementia, and was nonverbal, though she would hum. Her husband told me that he didn't think she would be able to play games because he didn't think she knew her colors or her numbers anymore. I recommended a game called *Thumbs Up*. While playing, she was putting the colored rings on his thumb, which meant that she was not only trying to find the colors, she was also engaging with him with physical touch. Oftentimes, late-stage dementia patients don't want to touch or be touched, so this was a big deal. All of a sudden, she stopped humming. She turned, and she looked at him, and she said "Do you remember? We used to have a cabin, and we used to play games." And he said, "We did," and he started to cry. She said "Oh, I loved playing games at the cabin." He took me aside later and told me that she hadn't spoken to him in two years.

People living with dementia often (but not always) regress in cognitive ability as the disease progresses. This not only takes away memories but the ability to speak, recall words, colors, shapes and numbers. This disease affects not only the person who is living with it – the isolation and stress often involved in caregiving can cause a decline in the emotional and physical health of the caregiver, too. Getting caregivers and family members to play games together can build and reinforce memories. Games that can be played as partners, such as *Timeline* where you can work together to answer trivia-based facts and insert them in a timeline of historical events and inventions, are best. *Yamslam* or *Double Shutter* are both dice-throwing games with limited decisions based on numbers, and they will keep everyone thinking. *Rainbow Rabbits* can be played as a two-player game by removing the speed element and helping players to create piles of cards discarded in rainbow color order.

It can also be helpful to play the classics with folks dealing with dementia – it can be comforting to hark back to their childhood, or memories of vacations or holiday games. The game *In the*

Palm of My Hand is based in a grandfather's memories through photographs. One player selects and manipulates objects in the palm of the other player's hand, trying to get them to pick the photograph of the memory being recreated. Be willing to help these individuals reconnect not just in memory but by touch, taste, smell and seeing, using all the senses to engage and unlock the family member lost in time.

Games can also be beneficial to folks facing cancer. Cancer can be the greatest battle of your life and the mental stress, along with the continued attack on the body, can leave a person unable to see a path to happiness. Focusing on laughter and light heartedness, party games that don't cause undue stress on the body are a great way to laugh and find joy with your loved ones. I can also recommend trivia games, word games like *Pick Two* and *Bananagrams*, dice games like *Pass the Pandas*, or *Roll For It*, and social deduction games such as *Love Letter*, or *Werewolf*. Roleplaying games that are world-building and focused on storytelling, like *Dungeons & Dragons*, have a higher barrier to entry, but once you learn how to play you can fight a dragon, go on an adventure or become a wizard without ever leaving your home. Roleplaying games are extremely good for growing imagination and offer a place to escape.

For many people, not just for people with learning and aging disabilities, games have a language barrier. The rules are hard to interpret and not accessible to all players. In 2018, I was pitched an idea by Jouni Jussila and Tomi Vainikka for an interactive app called Dized, which teaches how to play a game while playing, like having a friend at the table explaining the rules to you. I'm currently an investor and a member of the board of *Dized*. By using this technology, Dized is able to get people playing more games immediately. This app can be a game changer, literally.

Games improve your state of mind. They help improve your stress level and challenge your brain to a workout depending on the topic, style of play, mechanics of the game, and what an individual is naturally good at. Playing is essential and that was proven during the years of the pandemic. Play helped people socially, children learned skills that they were missing while being away from the classroom, and helped friends and families connect.

It was never in my life plan to be a business owner. I had to learn that skill in order to do what I loved – teaching people to play.

LYNN POTYEN *was born in Illinois and has lived in Sheboygan, Wisconsin, for the last twenty-six years with her husband Mark. They have three adult children – Erik, Rachel and Alex. Lynn opened The GameBoard in 2006 and in February of 2020 was nominated for the "Generations of Play, An Oral History" project, and was archived in the American Folklife Center at the Library of Congress. Her son Erik, who was the motivation for the business, graduated Cum Laude in 2022 with a bachelor's degree in computer science.*

You can find Lynn and her store at the-gameboard.com

THE POWER OF PLAY

Ian Livingstone

My life has mostly revolved around games. Those of you who know my name might know that I've been fortunate enough to have founded or been part of some very successful games companies during a career that spans five decades – both tabletop games and video games – but my love of games began long before that. Games have given me a lot, and I have learned a lot from them – most of all, that games and play are valuable in ways that people often don't understand.

Chicken Feed

Like everyone, I played games as a kid. These were card games and traditional board games and family games, like *Monopoly, Buccaneer, Formula 1,* and *Risk.* Even then, I knew there was something special about games, and I'd seek out the opportunity to play them whenever I could. At school, I made friends with people who were into Lambretta scooters, blues music and board games – including one Steve Jackson, who would go on to be my lifelong friend and long-time business partner. There wasn't a lot of choice back then, so we played what everybody else played, which was usually *Monopoly*. *Monopoly* was – and is – quite rudimentary in design compared to the games of today. It went on for too long and there was a large amount of luck involved and it was often frustrating, but it was what we had. For a bit of fun at school, I'd try to wind the other players up by not bothering to collect rent on the cheapest properties, like Whitechapel and Old Kent Road. I'd say the ground rent was "chicken feed" and this earned me my nickname at school: Feed.

Harsh Lessons

I earned another nickname at school – Ivan. This one was given to me by my Geography teacher, Roy Coleman. He gave everybody nicknames. He was a larger-than-life character. He didn't bully or patronize children like other teachers did at the time. He treated us all as individuals and he was the only teacher at school that I liked. Roy understood that children were naturally curious and wanted to learn, but were bored by the formal broadcast and knowledge recall model of education. It certainly didn't work for me. His method of teaching was based around contextual learning, applied knowledge, and making it an enjoyable experience.

Aside from Roy's lessons and time spent playing games with my friends, school was a painful experience – sometimes quite literally, as this was still in the days of corporal punishment. Our teachers each had their own weapon of choice. The chemistry teacher used Bunsen burner tubing, which he folded over into a nice little whip-like thing, and the music teacher used a steel rule. The PE teacher didn't have much imagination, so he just used a shoe, and the head teacher took pride in his cane. They didn't often need much of an excuse to give you a whack. This was all quite normal back then. Unsurprisingly, I didn't do very well at school, and left with just one A-level – in Geography, of course.

Lessons in Diplomacy

After leaving school, many of my friends (including my Games Workshop co-founders Steve Jackson and John Peake) went off to university. With only one A-level, I went to the Stockport College of Technology to do an HND in Business Studies and a Diploma in Marketing.

I spent a lot my time at college playing table tennis, cards and *Diplomacy*, which was the gamer's game of the era. It was a great game, but it caused huge arguments between some people who took it too seriously. As well as playing *Diplomacy* with friends, I also played it by mail, with games run by Don Turnbull through his play-by-mail magazine, *Albion*. Everyone would send their moves in to Don, who had on his wall homemade *Diplomacy* boards covered in pins to represent the player's armies. He'd adjudicate all the moves and post out the results. With the advent of the internet and technology, the world has changed exponentially in the last twenty-five years; it's easy to forget how we played games remotely back in the 60s and 70s. We were a network of players, all over the UK, connected by the mail. A game could take a year, playing by post, during which time you would be phoning other players to try to form an alliance to attack another player. For example, you might ask them to help you invade Italy, and in return you'd attack France together, or something like that. You would post off your orders and wait to get the results back in the post, only to find out that your so-called alliance partner had done the exact opposite because they'd already done a deal with the player you wanted to attack. It was the ultimate backstabbing game!

Around that time, some Avalon Hill and SPI wargames began to trickle over from the United States. There was a store in London called the General Trading Company, which imported them, but they were still very difficult to get hold of. The first Avalon Hill game I bought was *Stalingrad*, and then *Afrika Korps*. I played *Stalingrad* with Steve, one of us playing as the Germans and one as the Russians. *Stalingrad* and *Afrika Korps* were both hex-based games, which took forever just to set up. The graphics on the tokens were just numbers with a symbol, and then you'd move one counter here, another over there, and then attack, after which you'd have to consult the combat results tables. It seemed like fun at the time, but looking back, I realize it wasn't really. I have to confess that I haven't been near a hex-grid board game in decades!

Lessons in Business

Over the next few years, for one reason or another, Steve, John and I all found our way to London. The flat we shared, in Bolingbroke Road, West London, became the scene of regular "beer and board game" nights. Throughout this time, we were always on the lookout for new games to play. We'd hear about a new game from the States and spend ages trying to get hold of a copy. We'd find a new game but always want more, and we met other people who wanted more games to choose from as well. It was at that time, in January 1975, that we decided to set up a part-time business – Steve, John and I – to make and sell our own board games. We called the company Games Workshop.

I didn't know many people in 1975 who made or designed

games. This could have led us to believe that making a living from games would be difficult, but we didn't really see it that way. We were just keen to get involved no matter what. We never set out to make money. We set out to follow a dream, to turn a hobby into some sort of fledgling business. As players ourselves, we wanted to have some influence on the type of games that were being created and sold. When we set up Games Workshop, there were wargames available from Avalon Hill and SPI, but we got to hear about some new fantasy games which were totally different. They sounded amazing...

We began with our own range of traditional board games – high-quality versions, made from wood by John, who was quite a craftsman. But in June we had an opportunity come to us which was literally a game changer. Fortune would have it that we became the UK and European distributors of Dungeons & Dragons, following an order we placed for six copies of the game! We began selling D&D by mail order through our fanzine, Owl & Weasel. Dungeons & Dragons ushered in the genre of roleplaying games in which powerful storytelling and the imagination – natural human instincts – combined with the structure of a game. Dungeons & Dragons was a huge hit in the UK, just as it had been in the US, and around the world. Contrary to popular belief, this didn't happen overnight. It was very hand-to-mouth in the early days. John decided to leave Workshop, and Steve and I had to live in his van at one point. But slowly, mainly through word of mouth, *D&D* took off and we were able to open a tiny office at the back of an estate agent's office in 1976.

We launched a new magazine, *White Dwarf*, in 1977, and our mail order advert in the first issue included more than a hundred different titles. There were Avalon Hill games like *Acquire*, by the legendary Sid Sackson, as well as games like

Afrika Korps and *Stalingrad* in addition to Dungeons & Dragons and a large number of fantasy and science fiction games. We began publishing our own board games, notably Apocalypse: The Game of Nuclear Devastation which was an updated and slightly simplified version of a game called The Warlord by Mike Hayes, perhaps Steve's all-time favorite game. Over the next few years, we published more games, classics such as *Talisman, Battlecars, Judge Dredd, Fury of Dracula, Railway Rivals*, and *Warrior Knights*, and produced an English-language version of *DungeonQuest*.

We launched Citadel Miniatures in 1978 with Bryan Ansell as Managing Director, and of course it was Citadel that designed and published Warhammer, the key franchise on which the stellar growth of Games Workshop was built. We'd started out wanting to get into the industry and having some influence on the kinds of games that were out there, and now we were publishing some of our own personal favorites. We were actually living the dream.

The Games Night Club

In 1986, while I was still at Games Workshop, I set up the Games Night Club for my board game-playing friends which I continue to play in to this day. Steve and I were joined by friends Peter Molyneux (a legendary name in video games, and also a lifelong board gamer), Clive Robert, Sky Quin, and Mark Spangenthal. I wrote, and continue to write, the Games Night Club newsletter, now at issue #631, summarizing our gaming sessions with jokes and poking fun at the members. I also record the points scored on the night and at the end of the year the winner gets to keep the Pagoda Cup for the year. It's a spoof Gentlemen's Club newsletter with a circulation of six.

Reading and Learning

In 1981, while we were still running Games Workshop, Steve and I began writing The Warlock of Firetop Mountain, the first book in what would become the hugely successful *Fighting Fantasy* series of adventure gamebooks. Children loved our interactive books which combined a branching narrative with a combat system. The reader was the hero who made the choices. It wasn't a passive reading experience. It was all about the readers being empowered. Through Fighting Fantasy I learned a lot about the power of play.

Back in the 1980s, people saw games as trivial, at best, and it was not uncommon for people to view them as actually harmful. The Evangelical Alliance published a warning guide about Fighting Fantasy books; a worried housewife in deepest suburbia phoned a local radio station to say that, having read one of my books, her son levitated. Of course, that was great advertising – all the kids thought "Wow, for £1.50 you can fly!" There were newspaper and magazine articles warning about the dangers of children using their imaginations too much, which was ridiculous. There were petitions sent into Penguin Books by worried parents who wanted our books banned.

Even though Fighting Fantasy got a whole generation of children to read, gamebooks were not seen as "proper" books. Fortunately, some more enlightened teachers and parents were starting to get in touch, telling us that the *Fighting Fantasy* books improved literacy levels, were great for reluctant readers, great for encouraging creative writing and critical thinking because of the choices you have to make while playing through the books. Being involved in the story themselves gave children agency and they could see the consequence of their choices. *Fighting Fantasy* turned out to be a very compelling proposition for kids who otherwise might not have enjoyed reading. The gamification of reading with Fighting Fantasy gamebooks was eventually seen as being very positive.

Seeing the power of play in roleplaying games, gamebooks, board games and later, video games, really convinced me that games are good for you. It's common sense, really. Play is the first thing all children want to do, and they do it instinctively. There is no prescribed formula for play. Play is natural. Play in the broadest sense of the word, from building blocks to solving puzzles to playing board games or video games, is important. It allows us to have fun, but it also has deeper and more tangible cognitive benefits. Playing games combines a broad mix of problem-solving, decision making, intuitive learning, trial and error, logic, analysis, management, communication, risk-taking, planning, resource management and computational thinking.

IT Lessons

Steve and I sold our stake in Games Workshop and left the company in 1991. I decided to jump ship into the digital world video games. As Executive Chairman of Eidos, best known as the publisher of Lara Croft: *Tomb Raider*, I learned even more about the relationship between play and learning. Video games encourage creativity and curiosity. Games give continuous assessment and do not punish players for making mistakes. Simulation games are used as a training tool for pilots, surgeons, the armed forces and other professionals. Games should be seen as a contextual hub for learning.

Running Eidos, it became apparent that there was a shortage of software engineers, artists and animators in the UK, not just in the video games industry but in all digital industries. I talked to Ed Vaizey, the culture minister at time, and told him about the problem. He pushed it back to me and suggested I write a report for government and make some recommendations. He got the funding from NESTA who also provided two amazing researchers to help me with the writing of the report, Next Gen.

We started off by looking at ICT (Information and Communication Technology) education in universities, but soon realized the problem was actually starting much earlier. Schools were teaching kids how to use proprietary software like Word, PowerPoint and Excel, but weren't giving them any insight into how to create their own technology. These were children who would be playing video games and using the internet at home, but schools weren't giving them any idea how they could *make* a game or a website. It was effectively like teaching kids how to read but not how to write.

We detailed twenty recommendations in Next Gen, the main one being to have computer science in the national curriculum as an essential discipline. To its credit, the UK Government responded with a new Computing curriculum to replace ICT in 2014. But, needless to say, people started saying that what was really needed was a flagship school to demonstrate the new curriculum's potential. That was like a red rag to a bull to me.

The Livingstone Academy, Bournemouth

I made an application to the Department for Education for permission to open a new school. Whilst my application was well received, I was advised to partner with an Academy Trust to operate the school since I had no experience of running a school. I partnered with Aspirations Academies Trust and joined their board. The Livingstone Academy Bournemouth opened in 2021 and will be an all-through school. It will take five years to fill and will eventually have 1,500 children. It's not a private school, it's a state school for people living in the local area, some parts of which are quite disadvantaged.

The Livingstone Academy Bournemouth aims to ensure

children's learning is authentic, contextual and relevant. That means equipping them with skills as well as qualifications, know-how as well as knowledge, both IQ and EQ. They will need resilience and a "can do" mentality no matter what profession they enter.

The ethos of the school is about creativity, specifically digital creativity, with children also having a good Arts education. I believe we need to move children from the passenger seat of technology into the driver's seat to enable them to create as well as consume. Basically, it comes down to education which needs to be in sync with twenty-first century life. It is the combination of computer programming skills and creativity by which world-changing companies such as Google, Facebook and Twitter were built. In a world where computers define so much of how society works, from how we do business to how we enjoy ourselves, I would argue that computer literacy is "essential knowledge" for the twenty-first century, arguably on a par with literacy and numeracy.

We want the children to be "world-ready" and "work-ready." Robots and Artificial Intelligence are going to do the jobs that involve repetition so there's no point in teaching children like robots as they won't be able to compete with the real thing! We need to teach children how to think and give them problem-solving, critical thinking and creativity skills. If we encourage creativity and diverse thinking in children and give them an entrepreneurial and can-do mindset, and an understanding of the importance of being part of a team, they could become job makers rather than job seekers.

Opening the Livingstone Academy has been hugely rewarding for me personally, as I've been able to apply the principles of games-based learning to the curriculum which so resonates with Gen Z and Gen Alpha.

What Games Have Taught Me

From playing games with friends, from roleplaying games and *Fighting Fantasy* gamebooks, from parents and teachers, and working in the video games industry, I've learned so much about the power of play. Games-based learning simulates real world environments, adds context and naturally requires problem solving, decision making, intuitive learning, trial and error, logic, analysis, management, communication, risk-taking, planning, resource management and computational thinking. Games like Minecraft stimulate the imagination and naturally promote creativity, curiosity, learning, concentration and community. Games give the player continuous assessment and allow failure in a safe environment. There is strong evidence to suggest that games skills build life skills, and that playing games is actually good for you. So, let's not think our children will turn into zombies when they are playing games. The chances are that they are learning some useful life skills. Combined with digital-making skills they might even go on to become the next global tech giant!

SIR IAN LIVINGSTONE CBE *is a General Partner at Hiro Capital. He has been in the games industry for forty-eight years since founding the iconic* Warhammer *company Games Workshop in 1975 and co-creating* Fighting Fantasy *gamebooks in the 1980s before moving into the video games industry in the 1990s, where he served as Executive Chairman of* Lara Croft: Tomb Raider *publisher Eidos and later Chairman of Sumo Group.*

WINNING
AND
LOSING

LEARNING THE RULES

Edoardo Albert

I was halfway down the road, the crash of the front door slowly dying away behind me, when I realized that, perhaps, it was not just the children who might benefit from learning to play board games. In my – somewhat feeble – defense, I had been on the point of winning *Power: The Game* (a *Diplomacy* derivative with added tanks and missiles) when everyone else in the family ganged up on me and destroyed my army. Even so, given that I was one of the adults in the room, my reaction – announcing that I was never going to play with them ever again if they cheated like this and then storming out of the house, slamming the door behind me – was perhaps not likely to make an appearance in any manuals of good parenting. But I had been so close to winning...

I grew up in the 1970s, playing games by Avalon Hill and,

especially, Simulations Publications Inc (SPI). The coldest I have ever been in my life followed a trip to a games shop in Finchley, a north London suburb (there weren't many places you could buy these games back then), where I spent all my money only to realize, as I emerged into driving sleet, that I had spent my bus fare as well. The walk home took me an hour and a half, by which time I was soaked and frozen. But, as I lay in the bath trying to warm up, I decided it had been worth it: I had bought SPI's *World War 3* and *StarForce: Alpha Centauri*. Although I did not know it at the time, *StarForce* was the first science fiction wargame produced for the mass market; as an avid reader of Robert Heinlein I snapped it up. Six years later, when the Human League were top of the charts with "Love Action" and "Don't You Want Me," my game senses immediately pricked: in an early example of the expansion of geek culture, the band had named itself after one of the factions in *StarForce*. As for *World War 3*, one of my most vivid game-playing memories involved laboring through the two-hour setup of the game, only for my playing partner to launch his missiles in the first round and everything to be over within five minutes of the first move. Needless to say, after that I did not play *World War 3* as often as *StarForce*.

The Human League topping the charts coincided with life, and its various possibilities, shouldering gaming out of my life for twenty or so years. My old games were consigned to the attic where I forgot them. A large part of the new life was my marriage to my wife, Harriet, and our three children. Our oldest and youngest sons, Theo and Isaac, are autistic, with Matthew, the middle son, being the neurotypical filling in an autistic sandwich, a role which has its own challenges.

A child psychologist who helped us greatly with Isaac explained that an autism diagnosis is a bit like a three-legged stool: it requires evidence of social communication difficulties, sensory issues, and behavioral rigidity, although two out of three is enough for a diagnosis. But these symptoms are what a psychologist looks for in making a diagnosis; for the autistic person, the experience of autism is very different. Theo once came home from school and announced, "That's another theory down the drain." Turned out, he had been making hypotheses to try to explain the otherwise inexplicable behaviors of his peers. What for neurotypical people is intuitive was for Theo a matter of investigation. Imagine the strain of always having to work out when to speak and when to keep silent, whether to look someone in the eye or look away. This produces the north pole of autistic experience: anxiety. A constant, deep-level anxiety that you are getting everything wrong.

Our boys, Theo and Isaac, are both verbal, for which we are hugely grateful, although in Isaac's case he was past three and not speaking, babbling or imitating: the only sound he made was an ear-splitting squawking noise like an angry seagull. But in a vindication for the effectiveness of early interventions, Isaac was seen by a speech therapist who, in effect, taught him how to talk. Now, you can't shut him up.

The boys illustrate the fact that autism is a condition that plays out through a personality. Theo is more introverted and rule-oriented: when he was little, after being put to bed he could not get up until one of us came to tell him it was all right to get out of bed. Isaac, on the other hand, is an extrovert, a boy who comes alive in company while regarding rules as always up for negotiation. Both found school difficult and, often, isolating: friends were hard to come by and, in Theo's case in secondary school, impossible.

As parents, we were close to our wits' end. Then, one Saturday morning, we were wandering around London's Covent Garden shopping area when we saw a group of children gathered around some sort of demonstration. The boys wormed their way in to find a war-blasted science fiction landscape with tiny but exquisitely painted figures wielding blasters and fighting hideous monsters. We had stumbled upon a demonstration of *Warhammer 40,000*. The man running it, who we later learned was the manager of the Covent Garden Games Workshop store, was extraordinarily skilled at involving the watching children: within minutes my boys were marshalling their Space Marines against a horde of Tyranids. What's more, they won, in no small part because the GW man noticed that the father of one of the other children playing was cheating to help his daughter, so he subtly directed the outcome against him.

This was the beginning of my reacquaintance with the world of gaming. Of course, I had known about the explosion of computer games but, having stopped playing Avalon Hill and SPI games in the late 70s, I had no idea of the renaissance in board and tabletop games that had taken place in the 1990s and 2000s.

We tried *Warhammer* and 40K, but the painting was too fiddly for our children, and the rules were too complex for me (although we did have some excellent games with Space Marines shooting Orks with rules suspended and replaced by potato guns). Even this abortive attempt at playing games had shown us that the rules-based, organized system of a board game would be useful for our boys, being something definite and clear rather than the minefield of school friendships. We just had to find the right games.

I came across an advert for a games show, when I hadn't even known these existed. I soon discovered there were enough people interested in playing games to rent out the ExCel center in London. So, with the boys – Mum had decreed that a games show was definitely the occasion for some exclusive Dad time – we went along to Salute 2009. It was a revelation. We tried out game after game: *Descent, X-Wing, Tanks, Memoir '44,* and *Ticket to Ride.* Of these, *Ticket to Ride* proved the most immediate hit.

It's a bit of an autistic cliché but, since the age of two, Theo has been obsessed with trains. To give my wife a break, I would take Theo on the trains on Saturday morning, stop at a station, watch the trains run past, then go home again. His interest was fueled by the playground of his primary school standing alongside the East Coast Main Line, allowing him to watch the trains during play time. When we discovered a game that involved creating your own railway network, we entered his idea of gaming heaven. Indeed, having begun with *Ticket to Ride: Europe* we rapidly acquired the expansions, building railway networks in the UK, Germany, India, Switzerland, the Netherlands, and the Nordic Countries. The one edition we did not buy was the USA, as Theo, even at a young age, was dismissive of American railways. Each game was interspersed with Theo's thoughts – invariably accurate and informed – about the strengths and weaknesses of the relevant country's railway system and, once the game had concluded, Theo carefully drew out either the winning or the most interesting network.

But this is running ahead to the story's conclusion. Getting there required us to negotiate the problems of learning to win, learning to lose and, simply, learning the rules, as a family and in the wider world. Which was why me walking out in a rage when I lost a winning position in *Power: The Boardgame* was so important.

As I was slamming the door and storming down the road, my wife was explaining to the boys that it was not just them who found it difficult to accept losing. Sometimes grown-ups did too; sometimes their father messed up and got too upset when things did not go his way. So when, shamefaced but also still struggling against defiance, I returned home, I found the rest of them continuing with the game and, as I watched while they ignored me, I saw the boys also accept when they lost armies or the other players united against them with only the most minor of protests. The game had become more important – and more enjoyable – than the victory.

As we expanded our range of games, the rages that had accompanied earlier disputes about rules and their interpretation receded and laughter became a more frequent accompaniment to games than rage. Matthew turned into an all-too-capable general at *Memoir '44*, beating me regularly as he matured and I aged. When I first became a father, I read, in Augustine's *Confessions*, how his son was the one man in all the world Augustine would have had exceed him in all things: now I knew it was true. Theo, aside from his mastery of the various iterations of *Ticket to Ride*, had also become, in true autistic fashion, an expert on medieval history and proceeded to trounce me at Columbia Games' *Richard III: The Wars of the Roses*, sweetening my regular defeats by telling me the history and characters of the various protagonists. For his part, Isaac became a master of armored warfare in *Tanks*, aided by a truly preternatural ability to roll 6s.

Then Covid struck. We were confined to the house, save for our daily walk: Matthew had his GCSEs cancelled, Theo, having left school with only one A-level, was doing an apprenticeship which had become a few Zoom sessions a week, and Isaac was bouncing off walls – and the rest of us. It was a volatile situation in which we all felt powerless, because we were.

Which was where *Pandemic* proved a tonic. Getting it after the first couple of months of lockdown – games being now easily bought online rather than requiring a trek to distant shops – we began to play as if our future lives depended upon it. It might rank as what psychologists label magical thinking, but it was hard not to think that our future freedom depended upon us, together, defeating the game through its various levels. We played and we lost and the lockdown dragged on. We played and we lost and we slumped into lockdown stupor. We played and – we won. We won, and we won, and we won again.

Eventually, the first lockdown ended, and Theo applied for a job as a railway planner for Network Rail – and got it! As a critical job, he had to travel to Network Rail's headquarters in Milton Keynes every day, even when the country locked down again for a second and a third time, while his peers at school were cloistered in dormitories, seeing lectures online. At 21, he is the youngest specialist railway planner in the company.

Playing board games had taught my boys to accept defeat while planning for victory and, for Theo, the problem-solving inherent in them allowed him to master the intricacies of planning railway schedules in record-breaking time. My boys have exceeded me and nothing in this world has given me more joy.

EDOARDO ALBERT *is an author and historian, specializing in the Dark and Middle Ages. He has written eighteen books for publishers ranging from Granta and Birlinn to Black Library, with an equal mix of fiction and non-fiction titles. He has also written features for the* Sunday Times, Time Out, History Today, History of War *and many other newspapers and magazines.*

KEEPING SCORE

Alessio Cavatore

Be warned: this might seem like a bit of a rant. It's something I've wanted to write for a long time – about the way we all (myself included) sometimes pass judgment on other people's designs, and I decided it was finally time to let it all out. But I will try to be constructive. Let me tell you a story about a board game I designed, and the comments I've read about it, and how they made me feel. And the lessons I've learned, which I want to share with you.

In distant 2015, for the first time in my career, I got to design a board game from the ground up as the lead (and sole!) designer – it was the Jim Henson's *Labyrinth* board game. You see, that movie has had a huge significance in my life (and in those of many others, I found out later). So, when the Jim Henson Company agreed to give my company, River Horse, the license to publish that game, I was over the moon (and still am, to be honest). Designing *Labyrinth* the board game was a labor of love. First of all, I decided it was going to be a family game, because I wanted to playtest it and enjoy it with my daughter, who was seven at the time. I wanted to pass on and share with her the enchanting atmosphere of the magical world portrayed by the film and its music (thanks again, Jim Henson and David Bowie), as well as its powerful message about self-reliance.

Imagining the game being played by parents with their kids, I decided on a cooperative design, and the fact that the story portrays a group of four characters on a quest was perfect for that. It also had the added bonus that the board game can be played solo – after all, you could argue that the entire movie happens inside the head of Sarah, the main character.

To represent the continuously changing nature of the Labyrinth, which is more of a mindscape than a real place, I decided that a system where the characters moved around a board with cards randomly determining what each board location was going to be would ensure that exploring the Labyrinth was different every time you played. Also, each card was going to be one of the creatures, encounters, riddles and traps that Sarah and her friends face in the movie, in a "scene-by-scene" approach. Each challenge is easier to resolve as a group, so finding your friends and banding together is essential in the early stages of the game and useful throughout. Except, of course, for the final challenge against the Goblin King, who Sarah must face alone, because "that's how it's done."

Getting the game to last only thirteen turns (as Sarah has thirteen hours to save her brother from turning into a goblin) was great for pace and game duration, but it was very difficult to design, given the many variables. After much playtesting,

I got it to a reasonable level of challenge, where a group of players that work together well should manage to defeat the Goblin King in time, but invariably when there is very little time left on the clock. And I added some variants to increase or decrease the difficulty too, for groups that preferred more or less of a challenge.

Finally, the game was released, and it was (and still is) a commercial success. I was overjoyed that so many people seemed to share my love for *Labyrinth*! The Facebook group we created was amazing – twenty thousand people sharing their stories, their pictures, their passion for this film, both related to the board game and not. I see myself as a solid miniature wargame designer – which is what I had been best known for up until that point – but then I thought: "Maybe I'm not that bad as a board game designer either!" Happy days.

Then I started noticing a few negative posts about the game, and looking into those I checked the BoardGameGeek entry. Frankly, I was shocked. There were hundreds of ratings, with an average score 5.3. Even worse, there were so many comments that were incredibly negative, often quite aggressive and rude. Reading through these was very disheartening and badly sapped my confidence. On the other hand, when voicing my sadness to a friend, he said that he had seen some very positive reviews of the game just recently, when he was buying it online as a present. And then he showed me the Amazon reviews of the game. Once again, hundreds and hundreds of ratings, but this time with a score of 4.7 out of 5! And these reviews were completely different, very positive – a blessing for my battered morale.

To give you an idea, the average BoardGameGeek comment was about the game being simplistic and old fashioned ("Roll-and-move? In this day and age? Outrageous!"), while the average Amazon comment was more like, "Feels like being in the movie – it was a blast playing it with the kids!"

The marked difference in score and vibe between these two websites taught me an important lesson. A lesson that I already knew on a rational level, but which suddenly became very real and visceral – as they say, you learn more from a little experience than from any amount of theory. There and then, I felt on my skin how differently a game can be judged by a different audience. (This, of course, applies to novels, films, comics, art, not just games – basically any form of creative endeavor.)

Painfully, I tried my best to learn anything that could be learned from those very different types of feedback. I concluded that my *Labyrinth* game is definitely not for the "serious gamers." It is not a game for those who want a lot of thinking and very little or no randomness.

Rather, it is for families and fans of the movie. A game for people who want to roll dice and have a laugh while exploring the colorful world created by Jim Henson, which is above all full of humor and has, in my opinion, the great virtue of not taking itself seriously.

And indeed, I reflected, that was my original intent – a game steeped in love for the subject matter and that I could enjoy with my wife and my seven year-old daughter. I thought that perhaps the game's age recommendation of 6+ would make that evident to the buyer, but perhaps we could have made it more evident on the packaging, perhaps having a picture of a family, with young kids playing the game, on the back of the box. Maybe we should have used the word "family" more prominently in the blurb, or made more careful choices of marketing media and venues. There were so many lessons to be learned.

Funnily enough, I also noticed that some of the very positive comments on Amazon did, however, hint at the fact that the game was a little too complex. Another important revelation. Because I am a geek, I ended up designing a game that is aimed at a family audience including many non-gamers, but that uses a level of rules complexity that is of course based on my experience of being a gamer. In hindsight, I can see that the game tries to appeal to both crowds, and should probably have been more clearly focused on either one or the other!

Well, we made sure to take that learning on board when we designed the *Labyrinth* roleplaying game. Though still very simple, that one is definitely a game for gamers, if nothing else by the very nature of being a roleplaying game, a format that is (still) nowhere near as mainstream as board games.

On the other end of the spectrum, if I were to make a new edition of the *Labyrinth* board game, I would simplify its rules even further, making it even more accessible to the "right audience."

All in all, this experience taught me a very important business lesson about having a clear audience for your designs, rather than trying to kill too many birds with the same stone. But there was also another important lesson – a personal one. One that I learned for myself, and I'd like to share with you. A "lesson" sounds pompous, though... so let's call it a plea.

Please, when expressing judgment on someone else's design, let's all try to be kind. For me it's all about the difference between "This game is bad!" and "This game is not for me."

I have in the past made strong remarks about a design I did not like. And then I realized I knew well the people involved in that design, and I'm sure they tried as hard as they could to make the final product as good as possible. Who was I to judge their levels of motivation and efforts? How much did I know of the many, often private, difficulties they faced during the design process? And above all, had I recognized that, while I might not like their design, I might be completely the wrong audience, and their design would bring many hours of fun and enjoyment to other people that simply had different tastes or needs than mine?

So, now I always try to caveat any judgment I'm asked to make with the words "in my opinion," "to my taste," "for me," "this does not work for me," or "it's not for me, but…" I think that reading comments with these kinds of tags help the author or the designer to understand, accept and perhaps welcome the feedback. Most importantly, it should help to avoid hurting their feelings too badly. (Not that many people seem to care about other people's feelings on social media.)

Also, it's worth keeping in mind that if feedback is presented politely and respectfully, it is more effective. We are naturally defensive of our designs, and an aggressive, rude comment will normally not be accepted, no matter how true. So, even if your intent is not to be kind, but just to ensure that your feedback is heard, being respectful always helps.

Experience has taught me that as a games designer you should always be very clear from the very start about the audience for your design, keep that audience in mind during development, and make sure the final product unequivocally communicates the intended audience to your customers. Don't try to please everybody. You can't. The world is full of different kinds of gamers – some like chess, some prefer *Monopoly*… and everything in between.

I hope I've taken onboard these lessons about having a clear target audience and applied them to my next board game, *Noli*. This game is very much targeted at families playing together in terms of feel and rules, and intentionally made small in terms of components, as we imagine the game being played on a bar, a beach towel, or a folding camping table while on holiday!

This is also another game which is very dear to me personally, being based upon the folklore and traditions of a small town in Italy, where I spent my summers as a child.

So, for all these reasons, be kind when passing judgment on someone else's design. Remember that the game you're judging might just not have been developed with you and your tastes in mind. Don't think you are the repository of the ultimate truth, even if you are a genuine expert.

Ultimately, of course, there is an alternative approach to the above, which is where the wisdom of the older generations comes in. Just like my grandma taught me: "If you have nothing kind to say, say nothing at all."

ALESSIO CAVATORE *is an Italian-British games designer and entrepreneur. He founded River Horse in 2010, to produce board games, miniature games, card games and roleplaying games, including* Shuuro, Labyrinth, Noli *and more. Prior to that, he worked for fourteen years at Games Workshop, serving at one time or another as lead designer for all three of Games Workshop's core game systems (*Warhammer, Warhammer 40,000 *and* The Lord of the Rings Strategy Battle Game*). In his spare time, he sometimes likes to rant.*

You can find Alessio and his games at riverhorsegames.com

MORE THAN THE GAME ON THE TABLE

Susan McKinley Ross

I think most gamers know that when you play a game with someone – much like when you bake or hike or craft with someone – it's about more than the game on the table. It's about the time you're spending together, the way you're interacting, and the memories you're making.

I've loved playing games since I was a kid. My mom's side of the family regularly played games after dinner. When I was six, they taught me how to play whist, a simplified version of bridge. I loved getting to play what seemed like an adult game. My mom and my grandparents treated me like a peer when we played whist, and that was pretty thrilling for six-year-old me.

My mom and I were always partners, playing against her

parents. I adored sitting across the table from my mom and getting to be her partner. Everyone in my family was competitive, but friendly competitive. We were the kind of competitive where it is a natural and fun part of the game to compliment your opponents on a good play. After each round we'd talk about the hands we had been dealt and the chances we did or didn't take and how that paid off. We enjoyed playing the game together more than we enjoyed the game itself. This experience set the tone for my gaming life – games are great, but the people I play with are the best part of playing games.

As I got older, my family played a lot of *Scrabble*. Inside the lid of our *Scrabble* box we kept a running list of words that we decided to accept, and the date when the words were added to our family *Scrabble* lexicon. We had fun debating the validity of a word and we usually erred on the side of allowing words that gave someone a big score. This house rule was part of how I learned that it is not just acceptable, but valuable to modify the rules of a game to fit the needs of the players. I think knowing this made it easier for me to modify other games, and eventually to become a game designer.

One summer, my grandma and I played gin rummy so often that we left our favorite worn-out deck of cards on the dining room table, ready for us to play whenever we wanted. I still love the rhythm of mini-victories that comprise gin rummy – the joy of getting the card you've been waiting for, making a run, or taking a great stack of cards from the discard pile. My grandma would take breaks throughout the day to sit at the dining room table and play gin rummy with me.

I didn't fully appreciate our summer-long gin rummy-a-thon when it was happening, but now that I'm a parent, I realize how blessed I am that my grandma enjoyed playing gin rummy endlessly with me. I see those hours we spent together as an enormous gift of love. The soft worn-out deck of cards we used goes on my Dia de los Muertos altar every year.

Games were also important on my dad's side of the family. My dad and my grandpa played cribbage for bragging rights. It was serious. Almost as soon as I learned to play cribbage, I jumped right into the rivalry. Whenever two of us got together, the cribbage board came out. After we played, we would call the third person and let them know who had won. Even though it was intensely competitive, what I remember most is my grandpa's face completely scrunched up with laughter and my dad's face beaming. I don't remember any specific wins or losses – just the fun of playing cutthroat with good opponents who nonetheless laughed a lot.

My grandma refused to learn how to play cribbage. She wisely chose not to engage in that level of competition with her husband. Near the end of his life, my grandpa had Alzheimer's. He wanted to play cribbage, but he couldn't do it on his own. And so, after more than fifty years of marriage, my grandma learned to play. I can picture my broad-shouldered grandpa sitting down while my grandma stood behind him, leaning over his shoulder to show him which card to play. It was a hard time for everyone, but she lovingly offered him the comfort of cribbage at a time when he couldn't quite manage it on his own. My grandpa's cribbage board also goes on my Dia de los Muertos altar every year.

One Christmas vacation during college, I came home very sick with what I think I turned out to be bronchitis. I was determined to get up and do things anyway, but my mom knew I needed to rest, so she gave me an early Christmas present to open. It was a book I desperately wanted to read. I stayed home, reading on the couch that whole day. The next day I was once again adamant that I needed to go out in the world.

She gave me another early Christmas present to open. It was a fancy *Scrabble* game with its own revolving board. We spent that whole day playing *Scrabble*. I rested, I didn't go out, and I got better. It's pretty sweet that my mom used books and games to take such good care of me.

My husband Chris and I both love board games and we started hosting a monthly game night in 1998. Way back then it was a small group of friends and a very small selection of games. We'd get together at Chris' apartment on a Saturday night, eat snacks from Trader Joe's, and stay up way too late playing whatever games we had. I think we once stayed up until 4:00 AM playing *Honor of the Samurai*. Over time our group of gaming friends and our game collection grew.

Our game night keeps us connected with some of our best friends – and motivates us to get our house clean enough for company at least once a month. There are friends who come every time and friends who come once a year. As people arrive, we all stand around our kitchen eating snacks and chatting. Then we randomize into small groups. Each group makes a stack of six games they are interested in playing and then they roll a really big yellow foam die to decide which of those games they'll play.

We sit down to play a game and when the game is over, we chat some more. Eventually we figure out if we should wait for another game to finish so we can randomize people again. Our friends are awesome, and everyone drifts between playing games and chatting. Many of us have been playing games together for years. There's an ease and a comfort in playing games with the same great people regularly – game night is a lot like playing after dinner games with my family when I was growing up.

Our friend Greg was an early and integral part of our game night. For many years, he drove an hour each way to game night. He organized celebrations for our five-year game night anniversary and our ten-year game night anniversary – including getting us the really big yellow foam die. He'd often come early to help us set up. He usually brought delicious donut holes or homemade brownies to share. His eyes would sparkle when he made a really good move in a game.

Greg died in June 2019. I burst into tears at our next game night because it felt so wrong for him to not be there. If it weren't for his dedication to game night, we would have only seen him a few times per year. I am grateful for the time we got to spend playing games together and for the time we got to spend hanging out between games. I am grateful that I remember his laugh and that I remember the serious look on his face as he concentrated on a game. I'm grateful for the time he joined us for a *Lost Cities* tournament on our back porch. I'm grateful for his thoughtful comments as a playtester on my games, and that playing games helped keep us close. Thanks for coming to game night, Greg. We miss you.

Cooperative games and party games have given me some especially good game memories. Cooperative games nurture an entirely different feeling than competitive games. We like to play cooperative games at the end of our game night because they often help us end the night on a high note. Once we were playing *Dominion* with my brother and sister and there happened to be way too many attack cards in the mix. When *Dominion* was over, Chris and I suggested we play *Forbidden Island* as a palette cleanser. And it worked! The stress and frustration that we felt after a super-attacky game was slowly eased away by the cooperative game. It put all of us back in an agreeable mood. I think my mom and grandparents would have seriously enjoyed playing *Forbidden Island* after dinner.

Party games are a special – and kind of magical – subset of board games. Party games can make everyone laugh hysterically over the silliest things. The first time we played *Telestrations*, Chris misinterpreted water buffalo as "wave bison" and we both still think that's way funnier than it actually is. Our *Pictionary* box has drawings saved from years ago because the guesses were so funny. We were playing *Catch Phrase* at a birthday party once and a slightly tipsy friend ran in circles trying to get us to guess a word. I cannot remember the word he was trying to get us to guess – but I will never forget his frantic circle run as the entire room laughed hysterically. *Apples to Apples*, *Dixit*, *Just One*, *Scattegories* – these games have brought moments of pure joy to me, my family, and my friends.

When I first started designing *Qwirkle*, I made a prototype and played it against myself many times. Eventually I liked the game enough that I wanted to play it with someone else. But it was my first game design, and I was very nervous about showing it to anyone. So, I took it to my mom. I'd spent my whole life playing games with her. I knew she was an astute player. But I also knew she was totally prejudiced in my favor, and she tended to be excited about everything I designed. There was minimal risk that she would dislike my game. And, in fact, she loved *Qwirkle* from the start. My mom would like you to know that she won the very first game of *Qwirkle* – seriously, she considered getting a t-shirt made that said exactly that.

My mom's encouragement was a driving force in the development of *Qwirkle*. Way before I even submitted *Qwirkle* to a publisher, my mom told me it would sell a million copies. That's lovely. That's what your wildly enthusiastic mom tells you and it feels great, even though you know it's totally unrealistic. But my mom was right. *Qwirkle* has sold five million copies. Thanks for the encouragement, Mom! I love you!

After helping me with *Qwirkle*, my mom became my regular playtesting partner. She always appreciated and praised the best parts of my designs – playing with her helped me build up the good parts of my games before I worried too much about the bad parts of my games. This turned out to be an integral part of how I design games.

My mom was amazingly laid back about me constantly changing the rules of my games. We'd go out to lunch together once a week. We'd split a pizza and a salad or a garden burger and fries. Both the pizza place and the burger joint knew us and knew our order. I'd bring whatever game I was working on. We'd eat lunch and we'd play. Sometimes I would change the rules mid-game. And it simply didn't bother her. She enjoyed helping me solve the puzzle of how to make the game better.

Not surprisingly, my mom eventually came up with her own idea for a game. She wanted me to design a game that encouraged people to say nice things to each other. She imagined kids could play it at slumber parties. At her urging, I designed it and pitched it to a publisher. It was called *Say Something Nice*. The publisher liked the form factor I had come up with (prompts on popsicle sticks that you pulled out of a tall box), but they wanted different questions. Eventually that game morphed into *This or That*. It isn't exactly the game my mom envisioned, but I have used it many times to get groups of kids to enjoy learning about each other.

My husband Chris is my other regular playtesting partner. He worked as a level designer in video games at LucasArts for many years and he's good at switching between seeing the whole of a game and seeing the individual parts of a game.

His board game knowledge is broader than mine and it's really helpful to have him as a reference when I'm trying to brainstorm solutions to game design issues. He's encouraging about my work, but he also knows I want to find and improve the weak points of my designs. One of the most exciting moments in *Qwirkle*'s development was the first time Chris played it. As I watched him get really interested in the game, it gave me a big boost of confidence.

I'm not sure I'd be a gamer, let alone a game designer, if I hadn't grown up playing games with my family. I wouldn't know nearly as much about board game design if I hadn't spent years hosting a game night with my husband and playing games with our friends. My friends and family were the core playtesters for *Qwirkle* and all my other games. All these pieces of my life led to me designing games, but first they led to deep connections with some of my favorite people.

Every game I play offers me the chance to make memories, to learn, to laugh, to groan, to be gracious or helpful, to take risks. There's the chance to add to our family lore or to build on a friendship. There's so much more than just the game on the table.

SUSAN McKINLEY ROSS *is a game and toy designer best known for designing* Qwirkle. Qwirkle *has sold more than five million copies in 40 countries and won numerous awards, including the Spiel des Jahres. Susan's other games include* Skippity *and the cooperative children's game* Hoot Owl Hoot.

You can find Susan and her games at ideaduck.com

REFLECTIONS IN A SHINY THING: EVIL STEVIE LOOKS AT EVIL STEVIE

Steve Jackson

This topic is almost like saying "What ME means to me." I have been a gamer since at least 1970 and a game professional since 1976. I have seen gaming grow from an occasional pastime of college kids (which is what I was when I started) to a central part of modern culture.

To be sure, we've been gaming for tens of centuries. Games appear in museum collections covering periods back to Rome (they had polyhedra!), and we know of the existence of the

Great Game of Ur even though we have lost the original rules. Games mean a lot to a lot of people, and have for thousands of years. But they mean more now, to more people, than ever before in history.

What's that to me, personally? Just... *everything*. I'm now pushing seventy, but I still get to play games. GAMES! In fact, when I stop writing for the afternoon, it will be to play a game of *Iron Dragon*.[1]

A Life Well Wasted

What has gaming done for (and to) my own life? Not much... just *totally shaped it*.

The first game I ever wrote was *Ogre*, a tactical science fiction game that is still in print. It was commissioned as a licensed product based on Keith Laumer's classic *Bolo* stories, but the publisher ended up chickening out and asking if I could scratch off the serial numbers and save him the licensing fee. I told him that I would have to change *everything* except the general idea of a supertank, and then, having made the appropriate show of reluctance and dismay, I wrote the game I really wanted to write – one that set up quickly, played quickly, and could *not* have been a legitimate development of Laumer's work. When I saw that I could make up my own story, I never looked back.[2]

The *second* game I ever wrote was *Melee*, a simulation of medieval combat on a man-to-man scale.[3] I wanted some

---

1 I lost. Badly. And had a great time.
2 Though I have, since then, had the privilege of working within some amazing worlds created by others, and that's a kick too. But if anybody asks me, I recommend starting with your own original work, and only touching the worlds of the masters after you know the craft.
3 This is now a free download at www.warehouse23.com – log in, and search for *Melee*.

semblance of realism and wasn't satisfied with the research material I could find, so I joined the Society for Creative Anachronism (SCA) to practice with real (padded) weapons and learn some tactics. The SCA was so much fun that I remained active for years; that's where I met the love of my life. (She later came to work for SJ Games, and helped enormously with *Munchkin*, and I miss her so much – and without games, we never would have met.)

I'm also a science fiction fan. I love to read and I love to go to conventions. I used to write articles and reviews for SF zines, I used to help run cons, and I *still* write stupid filk songs.[4] But it wasn't my contributions to fandom that got me invited to be a guest at the World Science Fiction Convention in Dublin. Nope, it was my notoriety as a game designer. So gaming got me that completely unforgettable experience.

I've been able to cross gaming over with my big personal hobby, building with Lego, by writing *Evil Stevie's Pirate Game*. If that title intrigues you, *ESPG* is available for free. It is basically a tactical ship-combat game in which grown-ups[5] crawl around on the floor, yelling "Arrr!" and pushing minifig-scale pirate ships.[6] After a hiatus of nearly fifteen years, I got to run *ESPG* again at the Summer 2023 Brick Rodeo convention, and it was just as much fun as I remembered. Therefore, the version you will find online is newly updated for faster play, less rules-checking, and more sailing around and yelling "Arrr!"

---

4   A "filk" is a science fiction or fantasy song, possibly with original music, but more likely written to the tune of something your audience will know and sing with.

5   Mostly grown-ups. You need a child to play the sharks.

6   You can find it at sj.sjgames.com/PirateGame

Image: Steve Jackson

Gaming saved me from having to find honest work. It quickly went from a part-time gig, to an excuse to drop out of law school,[7] to a career that paid the bills! I can *write and play games* and make a decent living. If that's not meaningful, I don't know what is!

Gaming lets me feel like I'm giving back, not just to my fellow gamers, but to the world. Steve Jackson Games employs thirty-five people; a drop in the bucket, but with enough drops

---

7   Long story. I would have been good at it. And I really recommend courses in Contracts and Legislation if you want to write good rules. But you would not have liked Lawyer Stevie.

like that, everyone in the world would get three meals a day.

Gaming is good for me. I'm an introvert by nature. I most easily open up at the game table or talking about games. And gaming forces me to *keep up with the world* instead of crawling into a hole with a book, let alone some kind of internet echo chamber. It has made me a more rounded person.

I'm an introvert, yeah, but a competitive one. And it could have gone in an unhealthy direction. I'm a little bit smart and not even a little bit modest. But games let me channel my competitiveness and work on both "co-opetition" and the group competitiveness of a team working to beat a challenge. And gaming lets me *not* always be the smartest person in the room. I regularly meet people who can beat the pants off of me at games X, Y, Z, and *Puerto Rico*.

Game theory, of course, has existed for a long time, but academic study of "gaming as we know it" is new. A great deal of what I think I know about game design has been self-taught, for better or worse. But I now have the privilege of passing on some of what I've learned, and that is just inexpressibly cool. In essays like this, and interactions with game designers of later generations, I can explore what I'm doing, share it, and learn more just by watching *myself.* I compare myself to the blind zen archer. I don't always know what I'm aiming at, but I seem to hit it pretty often. Our next generation of writers and designers will have better arrows and eyes wide open.

Board gaming isn't going away. It's solidly entrenched in our culture now, a popular way to interact with your friends, and meet new people, for low stakes, which makes it a great way to make friends. Not *no* stakes… when a pastime has no stakes at all, it's less meaningful. But *high* stakes are stressy! I'm not a poker player; I get enough gambling by owning a small business. Which leads us to…

The Business of Fun and the Fun of Business

I've also learned a lot about business since I sort of fell into it. Some of it was from my first publisher.[8] The great majority was from the School of Hard Knocks, South Austin Campus, chief instructor Joyce L Jackson – my mother, my best-ever CFO, and my business coach for many decades. It turns out that the game business and game publishing make up a game about games – a metagame, if you will. (Those who know, know.) And that metagame has been my life for forty years and counting.

We get back to competitiveness and cooperation again. I'm definitely competitive in business. I want to publish the best games,[9] be the most humane and healthy place for a gamer to work,[10] and make a metric ton of money.[11] And awards are nice too, though I'll agree with the old bromide – just being *nominated* is honor aplenty. I still have enough impostor syndrome that I'm thrilled when somebody asks for my autograph, even if they think I'm the other, British Games-Workshop-founding Steve Jackson! Or when a retailer or distributor, a person whose very living depends on their commercial judgment, orders my games.

But cooperation in business is vital. Bare is the back of a brotherless man! I don't just mean cooperation with other elements of the supply chain; I mean cooperation with your "competitors." Compete, sure, but do no harm, and do good when you can. At SJ Games, we work with "competitors" every day. We have shared advice about printers and distributors,

---

8   And some of that was wrong, like the injunction to never, ever borrow money.
9   Doing okay!
10 Trying, really trying, definitely beating the average!
11 I'll be sure to let you know if *that* happens.

granted licenses, taken licenses, borrowed money, loaned money, shared booths and shipping containers and facilities and staff time, hired staff away to give them promotions, had staff hired away from us to get promotions, the whole nine yards, and everybody won. This could turn into a long essay about effective cooperation in business, and I'm not going there, but I'm thinking it would be a wonderful and novel topic for a convention panel.

Looked at properly, the companies most similar to yours aren't truly your competitors at all, but your marketing partners. They are out there working to create a demand for your kind of game and raise its visibility against all the other things that aren't table games at all (Netflix, Nintendo, doomscrolling politics, whatever!) *You need them.* For example, Hasbro makes *D&D*, which has been responsible for more *Munchkin* sales than a hundred years of my own marketing budget.

A truism: in any business, your biggest assets are your people.[12] Nevertheless, some of the people you hire will turn out to be pond scum. Don't be embittered and turn into a bad boss for the *good* people. Be fair. Listen to what your employees say – by definition, they are closer to some things than you are. Pay isn't as great in the board game industry as, for instance, in videogames. Give the best benefits you can afford. And manage your business responsibly so you can offer consistency and security, rather than mass layoffs every other Christmas!

A side note: what if you yourself are a bad boss? Here we get back to "English is a tricky language." There's a difference between "bad" and "not good." The way not to be an *evil* boss

---

12 English is a tricky language. Don't think of "your people" the way you might think of "your car." Think of them the way you think of "your beating heart."

is just... don't be evil.[13] But you can be a purely lawful good-aligned character and still be bad at the job of bossing. The way not to be an ineffective or inattentive manager is to hire someone better than you are. I am a good organizer; it's part of writing good rules. I am *not* particularly good at being a *boss*, but some people are. So I ask them to do what they are good at, and I write more games.

Everything Old is New Again

All this history we are accumulating has a bad side effect – games can get lost. Even very good games! As our marketing director, Katie Duffy, put it: "When a company goes out of business, becomes a subsidiary or is broken up, there is a greater chance that the rights to its games and assets will be tangled up in legal disputes or otherwise lost. Beyond the mere entertainment factor, the loss of games also means a loss of unique rules, mechanics and other assets that could have inspired the game designers of today and tomorrow."

What about the internet? Doesn't everything stay recorded in the cloud forever? Oh, you sweet summer child. The cloud is not magic; it's a function of technology and economics. Cloud providers can go out of business too.

So what can we do? Well, the "you" part of "we" can be interested when someone brings out an old game. Newest is not always best.

And the "me" part of "we" can work to bring old games back to print. Recently we have republished *Wiz-War* and *Groo: The Game*, whose combined age is probably greater than mine. At Gen Con coming up, I hope to nail down the rights to another

---

13 Google clearly isn't using that motto anymore, so it is free for the taking. Try to do better with it than they did.

neglected classic. It's important to me that the really good stuff stays in print! (And yes, if it's really good, it will keep on making money for distributors, retailers, and publishers, and yes, that's a big win too.)

And both the "you" and "I" parts have to keep firmly in mind that not even the classics are perfect. I'd rather keep learning, and bring out new editions when they seem necessary, than reprint a game unchanged just because it was that way twenty years ago. The things we learn about game design can be applied to the classics as much as they can the new creations.

That applies to you, too. Nobody says you have to play the Rules As Written if you have a better idea. Don't think a game is quite right? Hack it: for ease of play, or for a greater challenge, or whatever else floats your boat.

And New Stuff is New, Too!
But the classics are to be protected, studied, and enjoyed – not worshiped. Most of all I am interested in the new. What are we going to add to our current idea of board gaming, and can I be a part of it?

Virtual tabletops were in their infancy ten years ago. If you ask me, they're still in their infancy; the full-featured ones are just too hard to use. But they will get there, and then the term "board game" will have a new and deeper meaning. Computers won't take over board gaming; they'll just provide a tool to let you play with your friends in Nairobi and Saskatchewan. Or, if you are the one who moves to Saskatchewan, you'll be able to keep all your gamer friends.

Streaming or canned how-to-play videos are now a fairly mature art, I think, and it's a wonderful way to supplement the rules with a good demo that you can watch in your living room any time you care to.

STL files and 3D printing will soon allow people to design and make their own playing pieces, easily and quickly. That will change the way miniature manufacturers do business, but it won't kill them; it will empower them to concentrate on skilled and varied sculpture.

Artificial intelligence will also play a role. Will it be to create art, to create text… to Gamemaster? The answer in all three cases is really "kind of." AI can create art that needs human intervention, unless your goal is simple abstraction. It can create text that needs human supervision, unless you want an occasional fling of wild inaccuracy. And it can already create great flavor text for a game, but it can't write an adventure. That's my job, and yours. So don't fear the AI. Train it and put it to work!

People ask me "Of all the games you've done, what is your favorite?" And sometimes I give a smart-ass answer like, "Of your children, which is your favorite?" But the true answer is *the one I'm working on now.* And my favorite year for games is the year that is just starting. Join me at the table?

STEVE JACKSON *has been designing games for forty-five years and has no intention of stopping. His creations include* Munchkin, Illuminati, *the* GURPS *and* Fantasy Trip *roleplaying systems,* Ogre, Car Wars, *and* Zombie Dice. *He loves game, Lego, and SF conventions. He is a citizen of the internet until Texas cleans up its act.*

You can find out Steve and his games at sjgames.com

HUGS TO MY CHILDHOOD SELF

Fertessa Allyse Scott

From a young age, I loved playing board games, but the foundation of that love was built very slowly, brick by brick. My parents didn't believe in being idle so, from the time I could go to school, I was always doing something. From elementary school to high school I took part in all kinds of activities, including softball, basketball, youth gospel choir, art club, and a slew of other groups, none of which kept me particularly engaged. Despite being consistently active in these groups, I didn't usually make friends or have a sense of community.

It was at home that I was first introduced to board games. I only knew the mass market games that my parents would buy, or the older games my grandparents kept in the house. My grandad would play checkers with me, but he wouldn't hold back when he played, so that when I won, I knew that even as a kid I was just as capable as an adult. My mom would also play checkers and *Monopoly* with me, and when I cheated, she would leave the table and tell me exactly why she was leaving. Through her I learned it was never acceptable to cheat, and to only play games if I knew I could be a good sport when I lost.

Toward the end of elementary school, I became wrapped into Pokémania with all my classmates. We collected cards and unknowingly traded the best ones to older kids just to get the commons that we recognized from the show. We battled each other at recess, though battling was more like showing off our cards and making up the rules to the game.

As I aged into middle and then high school, it became harder to find people who would play board games with me. My parents didn't have as much time or patience to read the rules of the games they bought me other than a special occasion or two, and among my friends video games were king. My grandfather would still play card games with me from time to time, but mostly my gaming was relegated to playing *Monopoly* on the PlayStation, or sitting down with a classic board game and playing the role of two players until I inevitably won.

Monopoly was the one game I could automate since the movement was dependent on dice rolls, my strategy usually being to play one role as optimally as possible, and then playing the second player only mildly to my favor. *Monopoly* gets a bad rep in the hobby, but it was the one game that made me realize I cared about the human interaction in games rather than the game itself.

Instead of worrying about solving the puzzle a game gave me, I was more concerned with creating a moment within a game with the person I was playing with. This feeling was compounded in high school when I discovered the *Yu-Gi-Oh!* trading card game. Just like with *Pokémon*, the anime was popular among my peers, and we ran the halls shouting "GET READY TO D-D-D-D D-D-D-D-DUEL!!!" We wove the tallest of tales, each duel more grandiose than the last. It didn't matter who won or lost. It was all about the story, the ego, and the energy. Even though my dueling era came and went, my memories of the games we played together stick with me even now.

Eventually I graduated high school and went to college to study art. I joined more clubs and groups but was never quite able to find my place within them. My only contact with board games was playing *Yu-Gi-Oh!*, *Risk*, and a game of Spades with my family on the holidays. I started playing *Yu-Gi-Oh!* less and less. I only had one friend in college who played, and noticed my deck was getting more and more outdated. In college, I didn't have the money to keep up, and when most of my cards got banned, I put my deck away for good.

Video games, which had been crowned king in my childhood, retained the throne in college. If I went to a party or hung out with friends, that was usually what was used as the icebreaker. I had a couple of friends who introduced me to *Magic: The Gathering*, but it was on one of those bleary college nights where it was 3:00 or 4:00 AM, and I was more concerned with getting back to my dorm than learning this very intricate game. Once again, the hobby and I passed each other like ships in the night.

After graduation, I floundered for what felt like a long time as I tried to find my way to a creative career during a time now known as the Great Recession. I threw myself into job hunting, applying to literally hundreds of jobs right after college. A handful resulted in interviews, and a couple turned into internships, but nothing ever really panned out. A highlight during this time was a trip I took to visit my best friend from college. There was a lot about that visit that made me so happy, but my most vivid memory is my friend introducing me to *CATAN*. When we played it, my whole body lit up. It was near the end of the night, and everyone was tired, but I was so amazed that this game existed, and that I'd never known about it. I unfortunately had to leave the next morning, so I spent the next two years pining for a chance to play *CATAN* once again.

About five years after college, I finally found a job that let me move out on my own and, by extension, let me start thinking more about how I spent my time. By then, I'd made two new friends from a part-time job I'd worked, who also enjoyed games. They were the first friends I found who liked board games enough to commit to meeting up once a month to play them.

All three of us were just outside the hobby, so the games we played were the ones you would find at Target, like *Betrayal at House on the Hill* and *Sushi Go!*. We soon discovered Kickstarter, and realized there were a lot more games out there beyond those we saw on the shelf in big-box stores. We began to dip our toes into the rabbit hole that was hobby games, and it wasn't long before one of my friends said she wanted to create a board game. This was a turning point for me. My relationship with games had been very passive up to that moment. I had never considered that they were things that were created, nor thought about the people who created them.

I began thinking about what kind of board game I would make. I pondered it non-stop, from the drive home to the next day at work. I felt the stirrings of my dormant imagination, my mind buzzing with endless possibilities.

I went to work the next day still daydreaming about the possibility of my own game. I decided the theme would be about villains, because villains always had the coolest art and the coolest songs. Also, my friends always said I was up to no good when we played games, so I wanted a game where everyone had to be up to no good. That was how *Book of Villainy* was born.

I was so enraptured by the idea of this game that I skipped lunch to grab crafting supplies from the store to build my first prototype. It was very simple – a board with a track on it that had spaces with special effects. Very *Monopoly*-ish, to no one's surprise. I hadn't really learned much about game mechanics beyond roll and move yet.

Once the prototype for *Book of Villainy* was created, I was overtaken by the desire to play it, something completely familiar to me due to my childhood habits.

I broke that first game by testing it myself, seeing where my logic and the game logic divided. I saw questions that needed to be answered just by going through the motions. Why would a player do this? What if a player does that? They were the type of questions that only became obvious once I had something physical to move and solidify my ideas around. Everything seems sound when it stays in your head.

After self-testing, I made my first iteration, thrilled to have something I could bring to the next game meetup with my friends. I thought I would be satisfied having made a game that my friends could play, but their supportive feedback lit a fire in me. I started wondering how to make it better, and how to solve questions I'd never had to answer before. That was how I discovered the board game community.

One day on Google exposed me to BoardGameGeek, board game Twitter, and several prominent podcasts. I discovered thousands upon thousands of games I hadn't played yet, and a whole community of people who loved playing them. My journey to design one board game defied every doubt and weakness I had constrained myself with.

Compared to every group I'd joined before, the gaming community was responsive, even kind. People acknowledged me before even playing the game I'd created. And while I was still painfully awkward at initiating conversations, games bridged the gap for that as well. Instead of an empty exchange of business cards, networking felt much more natural. I would meet one person and that meeting would tumble to the next and the next.

I was constantly in a state of learning. I couldn't learn enough about board games, the different mechanics there were, and the various theories and opinions people had about them online. It amazed me that people thought about games with such depth, and it inspired me to do the same.

A long time ago one of my college professors said, "after college, no one will honestly give feedback about something you create." Board games defied that. With my first board game, *Book of Villainy*, I experienced the highs and lows of feedback and iteration. There were times when my game generated the exact moments I had been chasing from my childhood, with players cackling wildly at each other. There were other times where feedback was no longer constructive, it was insulting. Every iteration was an experiment, and every time someone was willing to play it, a joy. I learned how to take notes effectively, how to let go of my darlings while still hanging on to the identity of my game.

Growing up, I had been told to follow my dreams, and as an adult, encouraged to follow my passion, but up until 2017 I had lost my way. There had been many things I'd believed I was passionate about and, to be fair to myself, I cared quite deeply about those things. However, I had never been truly passionate about anything until I started working on my first board game.

My drive to bring that game to life overrode my need to be comfortable, time and time again. I went to board game conventions, often alone, surrounded by hundreds of strangers that I needed to convince to play my game over others. I went to many meetups and events where I was one of the few women and often one of the only persons of color, but still found the courage to stay even when I didn't feel welcome.

I found value in playing games I liked and value in the ones I didn't. When I played a game, I would analyze it and break down what did or didn't work for me, echoing the skills that college tried to instill into my creative process. Board games let me pick up all the pieces I'd dropped over the years to attain a job with a living wage. All the image and video editing software skills that I'd picked up in my internships, my creative writing, and my drawings all came back to help me on my game design journey.

I drew my characters, used Photoshop to create my board and cards, used video editing to make pitch videos and how-to-plays. My skills as an intern at a print store helped with making prototypes quickly and efficiently. The skills I had gained from my time as a quality control assistant helped me look at my rules and my prototypes with a critical eye. In turn, I contributed to the gaming community by offering that service for others.

Every odd job and skill got put to use, and for the first time in my life I felt myself operating at one hundred percent. I spent two years working on Book of Villainy, and against all odds was able to get it signed with a publisher. By that point I was completely enamored with board games and knew that I wouldn't stop at one. That next year I created and soon signed my second game, *Wicked & Wise*. Then, just as the pandemic hit, I was approached to co-create a party game, *Mansplaining*, which was also signed with a publisher within that year.

I ended up moving to Seattle to look for a job in the creative field, and was able to get a full-time position with Funko Games as a game producer. Game production is the project management aspect of game design, involving working to deadlines, keeping to a budget, and making sure your game develops with the correct audience in mind. I took on a dual role as both a producer and designer for nearly three years, living the dream of designing board games for a living, and it completely changed my quality of life.

Unexpectedly, I was laid off in 2023, but even then I was still very much surrounded by the warmth and grace of the board game community, in a city where tabletop games thrive. And while lamenting the loss of working with many I call friends, I was contacted by the many friends I'd made in the gaming community to help me with my job-searching endeavor. Thanks to that connection with the community and the experience I had gained along the way, I soon started working at The Pokémon Company International, a surreal childhood dream. My world is constantly shifting and changing, but what has remained is my passion for board games and the memories they create. I still feel the rush of excitement at the prospect of bringing a new game to life for no other reason than because I want to. Board games represent my coming of age, my passion, and my ability to move forward. They are the hug to my childhood self, reminding me that eventually I found my place and my people. They are the amplifiers that let me listen to my voice so I can walk my own path in life. They are the physical sum of my experiences and my love letters to the world.

FERTESSA ALLYSE SCOTT *is a game designer based in Seattle, where she currently works for The Pokémon Company International. She has designed and produced titles for Funko Games, including* Star Trek Cryptic *and the* Goofy Movie Game, *and as an independent designer she is also the creator of* Book of Villainy, Wicked & Wise *and* Mansplaining *(with Mondo Davis).*

Let the St🧸ries Inspire Your Moves

Endless Fun, Endless Memories:
Board Game Arena connects 9 million players from across the globe and offers over 700 classic and modern board games like **Ark Nova**, **Azul**, **Ticket to Ride**, and **Wingspan**.

Rediscover the joy of gaming with friends, family, and fellow enthusiasts, just as the book's stories remind us why we love games.

Ready to turn inspiration into action?
Join us on Board Game Arena today!
◀◀◀◀ SCAN NOW TO PLAY!

BOARD GAME ARENA

Play anytime, anywhere, and on any device – no downloads or installations need
It's hassle-free and easy to dive into the world of online board gaming.